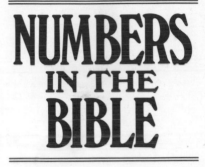

NUMBERS
IN THE
BIBLE

Robert D. Johnston

NUMBERS
IN THE
BIBLE

God's Unique Design
in Biblical Numbers

Robert D. Johnston

KREGEL PUBLICATIONS
Grand Rapids, Michigan 49501

Numbers in the Bible: God's Unique Design in Biblical Numbers, by Robert D. Johnston. Published in 1990 by Kregel Publications, a division of Kregel, Inc., P. O. Box 2607, Grand Rapids, MI 49501. First Kregel Publications edition: 1990. All rights reserved.

Library of Congress Cataloging-in-Publication Data

Johnston, Robert D. (Robert Dougall).
  [Arithmetic of Heaven]

  Numbers in the Bible: God's unique design in biblical numbers / Robert D. Johnston
      p.   cm.
  Previously published under the title: Arithmetic of heaven.
  1. Numbers in the Bible. I. Title.

BS680.N8J64   1990   220.6'8—dc20   90-36538
                                              CIP

ISBN   0-8254-3628-1 (pbk.)

3 4 5 Printing/Year 95 94

Printed in Colombia

Contents

Preface

In the great oceans there still remain parts whose waters have never been disturbed by the sounding line of the Navigator, and where "dark unfathomed caves" hold secrets in wonderful store. Across the far-flung expanses of the heavens dance myriads of stars which even the most powerful telescope has been unable to bring within the gaze of the Astronomer. And in spite of the diligent searching of man, an untold wealth of gems still lies hidden in the depths of the earth. So is it with the Word of God, which is the theme of the following pages, as they attempt to indicate something of its marvelous structure, particularly in the systematic use of numbers within it. While the subject matter is not new, it is by no means familiar to many devoted readers of the Scriptures.

Grateful thanks are expressed to Charles E. Stokes, M. A., for valuable corrections and suggestions. If some humble believer in God and His Word should receive help and encouragement from what has been written, the little labor entailed in the writing will have been amply repaid.

Robert D. Johnston

1

An Eternal Book

Ancient Eastern folklore tells of a fabulous bird, the phoenix. Having lived for five hundred years in Arabia, it built its own funeral pyre, and laying itself thereon, was reduced to ashes, out of which it rose again in the vigor of renewed youth. Thus it became to the ancients the symbol of immortality. The Bible, oftentimes laid by man upon the funeral pyre of worldly wisdom, and reduced by the scorching fires of criticism to a seeming heap of ashes, has, phoenix-like, as often risen again in the undiminished vigor of an eternal youth. There is one reason, and only one, which adequately accounts for this. It is that the Bible is the product, not of men, but of God, that its words are the very breathings of God (2 Tim. 3:16), words "which the Holy Spirit teacheth" (1 Cor. 2:13). Thus it is not merely the symbol of immortality, but immortality itself, the veritable "Word of God which liveth and abideth for ever" (1 Pet. 1:23).

It was at the dawn of man's history that the first critic, sire of an ever-increasing stock, began to sow the insidious seeds of doubt, when he broke the tranquility of that early scene with his suggestive question, "Yea, hath God said?" (Gen. 3:1). The attack then launched in this negative form by the "old Serpent, called the Devil" (Rev. 12:9), against the truth of God's Word, soon developed, and was repeated in positive form in these words: "Ye shall not surely die: For God doth know that in the day ye eat thereof, then your eyes shall be opened, and ye shall be as gods" (Gen. 3:4, 5). From that time till these present days, the attack has been continued unceasingly. Down through the centuries, the gales of opposition and infidelity have lashed themselves into a fury against this same Word, only to be spent in the effort, leaving the structure of Holy Scriptures intact as ever, not one single stone having been loosened, let alone dislodged from the foundation to the highest pinnacle.

The opposition of men to the Word of God is born of the fact that the Bible reveals man's sin, discounts his wisdom, makes his greatest might to seem puny, and lays his pride in the dust. As one has put it, "The Bible is such a Book as man could not write if he would, and would not write if he could." Towards this Book, he has shown the most intense hatred, revealing a determination to get rid of such a scathing indictment of his own depraved condition. To accomplish this, man after man has entered the lists against it. "Celsus tried with the brilliancy of his genius, and he failed. Then Porphyry tried it with the depth of his philosophy, and he failed. Lucien tried it with the keenness of his satire, and he failed. Then Diocletian came on the scene of action, and tried other weapons; he brought to bear against the Bible all the military and political power of the strongest empire the world ever knew, at the height of its glory. He issued edicts that every Bible should be burned, but that failed. Stronger edicts were issued, that those who owned Bibles should be put to death, and that failed. Every engine of destruction that human wisdom, human science, human philosophy, human wit, human satire, human force and human brutality could bring to bear against a book has been brought to bear against the Bible, and the Bible still stands" (Torrey).

Nor has this determined attack been confined to the earlier part of this era. In more recent times, the assault has lost nothing of its keenness. "In Hume, in Gibbon, in Voltaire, and La Place, not to mention a multitude of vulgar assailants, the Bible has had to sustain the assaults of the greatest talent, the sharpest wit, and the acutest intellects. To make it appear a cunningly-devised fable, philosophers have sought arguments amid the mysteries of science, and travelers amid the hoar remains of antiquity; for that purpose geologists have ransacked the bowels of the earth, and astronomers the stars of heaven; and yet after having sustained the most cunningly-devised and ably-executed assaults of eighteen hundred years, it still exists" (Guthrie).

This perpetuity of the Scriptures speaks loudly of their origin. What man can produce, man can destroy. But this Book, being the Word of God, partakes of the character of God, and has for its age immortality. However powerful the opposition to it may be, it is born but to perish, while the Book which is the object of its hatred is destined to be age-abiding. All that pertains to man the ravages of time will destroy; but the Bible is the Book of eternity. When the handiworks of man, the things upon which his fondest hopes are centered, and which he deems to be most enduring, have passed into oblivion, this Book will still abide; for the words of the Lord Jesus Christ concerning His own teachings are true of the whole Book: "Heaven and earth shall pass away, but My Words shall not pass away" (Matt. 24:35). And as it has been, so shall it be. "The empire of the Caesars is gone; the legions of Rome are moldering in the dust; the avalanches that Napoleon hurled upon Europe have melted away; the pride of the Pharaohs is fallen; the pyramids they räised to be their tombs are sinking every day in the desert sands; Tyre is a rock for bleaching fishermen's nets; Sidon has scarcely left a wreck behind; but the Word of God still survives. All things that threatened to extinguish it have only aided it; and it proves every day how transient is the noblest monument that man can build, how enduring is the least word that God has spoken. Tradition has dug for it a grave, intolerance has lighted for it many a fagot; many a Judas has betrayed it with a kiss; many a Peter has denied it with an oath; many a Demas has forsaken it; but the Word of God still endures" (Cumming).

How puny, then, is the opposition of men to the revelation of God, whether that opposition be from without in the form of loud-mouthed infidelity, armed as an avowed enemy, or from within, in the form of higher criticism, garbed as an apparent friend. Of the latter, which is by far the more subtle, the following aptly describes the value. The saintly Robert C. Chapman, of

Barnstaple, who passed to his reward in June, 1902, at the age of ninety-nine years, being asked his opinion of the modern criticism, replied thus in parable: "One day, while walking in the noonday light of a mid-summer sun, beneath a cloudless sky, I was accosted by a person wholly a stranger to me, who, with kind, condescending air, made offer to show me the way. I saw in his hand a lantern, and in it a lighted, farthing candle. Pity checked my rising laughter; so, as gravely as I could, I declined his offer, and went on my way. I was afterwards told that his name was 'Higher Criticism.'"

The relation between the Word of God and its critics in all generations, and the certain future of each, are described in these lines:

"Last eve I passed beside the blacksmith's door,
    And heard the anvil ring the vesper chime;
Then looking in, I saw upon the floor,
    Old hammers worn with use in former time.
'How many anvils have you had,' said I,
    'To wear and batter all these hammers so?'
'Just one,' said he, then said, with twinkling eye,
    'The anvil wears the hammers out, you know.'
Just so, I thought, the anvil of God's Word,
    For ages, sceptic blows have beat upon;
Yet though the noise of falling blows was heard,
    The anvil is unharmed, the hammers gone!"

Thus is being verified by the hand of Time, written large on the page of history, the very words of Scripture: "For all flesh is as grass, and all the glory of man as the flower of grass. The grass withereth, the flower thereof falleth away; but the Word of the Lord endureth for ever" (1 Pet. 1:24, 25).

2

An Inspired Book

"The Bible may be inspired, but so are the works of all good authors," is a common assertion of these days. Amongst certain classes pretending to a measure of culture, it has become fashionable to ascribe such works to the "inspiration of genius." But as the sun in his strength is to the most perfect mode of lighting devised by men, so is the Bible to any or all of the writings of men, superior beyond measure. No other book makes such claims as it makes. Scarcely have we commenced to read it, when we come upon the significant words, "God said" (Gen. 1:3). In its opening chapter the words are repeated ten times, and the same, or equivalent words, as, "Thus saith the Lord," abound throughout. In the first five books, according to Dr. Brookes, such expressions occur five hundred and one times, in the Historical books and in the Psalms two hundred and ninety-two times, and in the Prophets one thousand one hundred and eleven times. Thus with a total of one thousand nine hundred and four times is the Old Testament stamped with the mark of its Author. Of this Divinity of origin, its wonderful perpetuity is a convincing evidence.

It is by no means, however, the only evidence.

"How do you know the Bible is inspired?" was asked of a young man. Like a flash came the reply, "Because it inspires me!" A second manifestation, then, of the Divine origin of the Scriptures, is found in the power which they have wielded, and continue to wield, over the lives of men. Evidence of this nature defies every effort to refute it, but plants its feet firmly on the bed-rock of a personal experience, and gives the lie direct to all contradictions. As has been written: "The highest proof of the infallibility of Scripture is the practical one that we have found it so. As the coin of the realm has always been found to buy the amount represented on its face, so the prophecies and promises of Holy Scripture have yielded their face-value to those who have taken the pains to prove them." And with what result? Down through the ages comes the low hum of a multitude of assenting voices, increasing in volume with the passing of the years, till it bursts forth into a mighty thunder-roar of praise to God, each saying, "By the grace of God I am what I am" (1 Cor. 15:10), a grace enshrined and conveyed in these same Scriptures. The Book that alone possesses effective transforming power upon the lives of men, must of a truth be God's Book.

Besides these external evidences, many internal evidences manifest beyond question that "all Scripture is given by inspiration of God" (2 Tim. 3:16). Here is a collection of sixty-six books, produced in three different languages, Hebrew, Aramaic, and Greek, and comprising every form of literary structure. Over a period of fifteen centuries, some forty men, varied in their attainments as they were in social grades, living in lands separated by hundreds of miles, were used to write these books. Yet this Book displays at one and the same time a perfect progression of revealed truth, and an equally perfect, unbroken unity, which baffles human comprehension, and compels the admission of its claim to be God–breathed.

One has well put it in these words: "The authorship of this Book is wonderful. Here are words written by kings, by emperors, by princes, by poets, by sages, by philosophers, by fishermen, by statesmen, by men learned in the wisdom of Egypt, educated in the schools of Babylon, trained at the feet of rabbis in Jerusalem. It was written by men in exile, in the desert, and in shepherds' tents, in 'green pastures' and beside 'still waters.' Among its authors we find the tax-gatherer, the herdsman, the gatherer of sycamore-fruit; we find poor men, rich men, statesmen, preachers, exiles, captains, legislators, judges,—men of every grade and class. The authorship of this book is wonderful beyond all other books. It required fifteen hundred years to write it, and the man who wrote the closing pages had no communication with the man who commenced it. How did these men, writing independently, produce such a book?" (Hastings). Yes, how indeed!

The answer to this last question is given by these lines of the poet Dryden:

"Whence, but from heaven, could men unskilled in
    arts,
  In several ages born, and several parts,
 Weave such agreeing truths? or how, or why,
  Should all conspire to cheat us with a lie?

Unasked their pain, ungrateful their advice,
  Starving their gain, and martyrdom their price."

The only solution that meets the case is the one supplied by the Book itself: "The prophecy came not in old time by the will of man; but holy men of God spake, moved [or, borne along] by the Holy Spirit" (2 Pet. 1:21).

This unity, moreover, is not a mere surface unity, but lies deeply embedded, being woven into the very warp and woof of the Book. Throughout, its theme is one and continuous, the record of God's dealings with mankind. These are summed up in two representative men, the first, Adam, head of the earthly race; the second, the last Adam, the Lord from heaven, the Man Christ Jesus. Of these two, the Scriptures form the history, and the unity of the account is abundantly manifest in the opening and closing chapters of the Bible.

In the opening book, Genesis, the book of beginnings, we find the record of earth created (1:1), night created (1:5), seas created (1:10), sun and moon created (1:16, 17), and a garden prepared as man's home (2:8). We learn of the marriage of the first Adam (2:18-23), the first appearance, on this scene, of Satan (3:1), the sin of man with its train of sorrow and suffering (3:16, 17), the curse of sin (3:17), and, finally, man driven from his God-given heritage and from the Tree of Life (3:24). Then follow the choice of a man, Abraham, the birth of a nation, and, in the fullness of time, the ushering into the world of the Son of God, "made in the likeness of men" (Phil. 2:7). This peerless Person, as the Lamb of God, puts away sin by the sacrifice of Himself (Heb. 9:26). And what then?

Turn to the closing book, the Revelation, the book of unveiling, and read with wonder the counterpart of these opening verses. There we pierce the mist that screens the future, and see the earth passed away (21:1), no night there (22:5), no more sea (21:1), the sun no longer needed (22:5), and a city to be an eternal home (21:10). With increasing adoration we behold the glorious marriage of the last Adam celebrated (19:9), the final doom of the arch-enemy executed (20:10), no more sorrow (21:4), no more curse (22:3), and the wanderer, once driven from the Tree of Life, receiving the welcome of pardoning grace (22:2, 17).

In the words of Dr. A. T. Pierson: "As we compare the opening of Genesis with the close of Revelation, we find that we have been following the perimeter of a Golden Ring,— the two extremities of human history meet; from the Creation, and Eden, with the Fall, we have at last come to the New Creation, and Paradise, without a Fall." Such a unity is explained only by the divinely-revealed truth that the many and varied pens on earth employed in the production of the Holy Scriptures, were fully controlled by the one Pen-man, in heaven.

A last, and most convincing testimony to the Scriptures of both the Old and the New Testaments is found in their relation to the Lord Jesus Christ. Christ, "the Living Word," and the Bible, "the Written Word," are so inseparably bound together, that to loosen our hold on one, is to surrender the other. "The Written Word is the Living Word enfolded; the Living Word is the Written Word unfolded." Most apt it is that God is described as the One Who was, and is, and is to come (Rev. 11:17), for such a description covers the range of His Word. The Bible deals with "things which were," or history; with "things which are," or doctrine; and with "things which are to come," or prophecy. Similarly, the New Testament itself is comprised of these very divisions, the first being the Gospels and the Acts; the second, the Epistles; and the third, the Revelation. Thus does God identify Himself with the very form of His Word. So it is with the Lord Jesus Christ, who was "God manifest in the flesh" (1 Tim. 3:16).

Loyalty to the Person of Christ demands loyalty to the Scriptures. Conversely, a critical attitude to the Bible is a betrayal of the Christ of the Bible. A man is no more correct in his attitude to Jesus Christ, than he is to the Scriptures of Truth. This vital relationship between the Son of God, and the Word of God, has a two-fold aspect. It consists of, first, the testimony borne by the Scriptures to Christ, and second, the testimony of Christ to the Scriptures. Again, each in a fourfold way guarantees the accuracy of the other. As to the first, the testimony of the Scriptures to Christ, He Himself declared, concerning them, "They are they which testify of Me" (Jn. 5:39). This they did, first, foretelling the nature of His birth (Is. 7:14), the town of His birth (Mic. 5:2), and His worship at His birth (Is. 60:3). Second, they foresaw the gentleness of His Person (Is. 42:2), His zeal for His Father (Ps. 69:9), and His life-work (Is. 61:1-3). Third, they detailed with awesome accuracy His rejection (Is. 53:3), and violent death (Is. 53:8), betrayed by one of His disciples (Ps. 41:9) for thirty pieces of silver (Zech. 11:12). Fourth, they looked beyond the darkness, and beheld His resurrection, His ascension, and His undimmed glory (Ps. 16:10, 11; Is. 53:10, 11; Jude 14). And as surely as the unerring accuracy of most of these has been made plain, so shall the others, with many more, find a literal and complete fulfillment.

Again, the Lord Jesus Christ, the very embodiment of truth (Jn. 14:6), offered abundant testimony to the Scriptures. He did so, first, during His life among men. "Had ye believed Moses," said He on one occasion, "ye would have believed Me; for he wrote of Me" (Jn. 5:46). Second, He did so at His death, for of those seven sayings which fell from His gracious lips, as He hung between the malefactors, three were in the words of the Old Testament Scriptures. Again, after His resurrection, He continued to give clear testimony to these same Scriptures. Overtaking two disappointed disciples, pursuing their weary way back to Emmaus, what comfort has He to offer them? Luke supplies the answer: "Beginning at Moses, and all the prophets, He expounded unto them in all the Scriptures, the things concerning Himself" (Luke 24:27). And last, from the very presence of God, the "Living Word" confirmed the "Written Word," for we hear Him say, quoting from the prophet Isaiah (44:6 and 22:22): "Fear not, I am the First and the Last: I am He that liveth, and was dead; and, behold, I am alive for evermore, Amen; and have the keys of hell and of death" (Rev. 1:17, 18). The Book to which the One Who said, "I am the Truth," could offer such unqualified tribute, must of itself be very truth.

Little wonder is it that the late Dr. Horatius Bonar should thus write of it: "I should like to avow solemnly in these days, that after fifty years' study of prophetic subjects, I feel a vastly greater certainty as years roll on, with regard to the Divine authority, and verbal inspiration of the Word of God." Nor is it strange that Thomas Newberry, a scholar of no mean attainments, should give expression to these words: "As a result of a careful examination of the entire Scriptures in the originals, noticing and marking where necessary, every variation of tense and preposition, and the significance of words, the impression left on my mind is this,—not the difficulty of believing the entire inspiration of the Bible, but the impossibility of doubting it."

Indeed, such a Book is the Bible, that when one has bowed with awe before the majesty of its claims and assertions; has wondered as the passing of the years has transformed its prophecy into history; has marveled at the accuracy of its minutest details, there still remain unplumbed depths to be sounded, inexhaustible mines of wealth to be explored. Sometimes, of an evening, one has gazed up into the star-lit canopy of the heavens, overawed by the glorious display of the majesty of God, sharing the wonder of the Psalmist on the consideration of "His heavens, the work of His fingers" (Ps. 8:3); and, continuing to gaze, one has observed more and more stars come within the field of vision. So, gazing into the pages of Holy Scripture, likewise the work of His fingers, the more we look, the more its wondrous beauties unfold themselves to the eye of faith.

To thus gaze, as the Holy Spirit may enlighten us, at the wonders of the Word of God as displayed particularly in the use of number, is the purpose of these subsequent chapters; for the accomplishment of which purpose we unite with the Psalmist and pray: "Open Thou mine eyes, that I may behold wondrous things out of Thy Law" (Ps. 119:18).

3

Design in God's Works

Napoleon, on his way to Egypt, overheard one night a group of scholars on board ship discussing the existence of God. They demonstrated with entire satisfaction to themselves, that God was non-existent. Napoleon listened in silence, then, pointing to the star-bespangled heavens, said: "All very well, gentlemen, but who made these?"

All nature unites in testimony to the work of God the Creator, "Who hath measured the waters in the hollow of His hand; and meted out heaven with a span; and comprehended the dust of the earth in a measure, and weighed the mountains in scales, and the hills in a balance" (Is. 40:12). The magnitude and magnificence of the universe, the creation of the hand of God, staggers man's widest comprehension, and beggars his best description.

"What is the universe?" asks Dr. Cunningham Geikie, "Pray, tell us, you who make so free with it. Are you silent? It is wise to be so. Thought comes back from its farthest flight, and folds its wings, wearied and blinded by the splendor, while yet on the very verge of the shoreless and bottomless All. A few

fortunate guesses and surface reflections from
all-surrounding mystery, make up the known.
Yonder sweep ten thousand suns and systems,
circle beyond circle, each distant from the other
as ours from them,—round the pole of the
universe; and still beyond, float countless
galaxies, each filling a heaven of its own, but
shrunk, to us, into faint, telescopic light-clouds,
in infinite perspective. Bounds wholly fail. From
our highest scientific watch-tower, we have only
a poor contracted horizon on the bosom of the
illimitable. For all we know, from the farthest
nebula, irresolvable by us, there may stretch
another Infinite, lighted by million suns, the
glittering emperors of the starry kingdoms of
innumerable skies. Know the universe! O man,
what dost thou know!" Of a truth, "the works
of the Lord are great" (Ps. 111:2).

Yet while men often fail to see past the
majesty of nature to the majesty of nature's God,
they are swift to recognize the wonderful order
and plan of things, which order they term laws
of nature. What are these laws, however, but
the expression of the plan of God in the material
world, the manifestation of the precision and
arrangement which prevail in all His doings,
"whose way is perfect" (Ps. 18:30)? Upon all
His works, law and order is stamped, and signs
of definite, numerical schemes are everywhere
evident.

It is so in music. Sound is the product of
vibrations of the air, the frequency of vibrations
determining the pitch of the sound, whether low
or high. For each note of the scale, the number
of vibrations per second is a multiple of eleven,
while the difference in the number of vibrations

for each note is also a multiple of eleven. The scale itself consists of seven notes, between which swing the sweetest and the grandest melodies which the genius of man can produce.

The realm of art, too, is dominated by this number seven. Light, passing through a three-sided block of glass, is broken up into its component colors, which are seven in number, and form what is called the sun's spectrum. These same seven colors go to paint the glories of the rainbow, the light being broken up by the water-particles in the air; and to their limits all the Turners and Rembrandts are confined, whether for dazzling sun scenes or pictures of more somber hue. Moreover, as each different element radiates its own special color, those seven colors of the spectrum point to the seven-fold composition of the sun itself.

The very structure of the earth's crust, as divided up by the geologist, pays its tribute to the wonderful plan of the Creator God. That crust is composed of layers, or strata of rock, the term rock, in geology, being inclusive of all materials, hard or otherwise, forming the crust. In its nature it is twofold, that which is volcanic in origin, and was produced by fire, or Igneous rock; and that which was laid down by the pressure of water, or Aqueous rock. Igneous rocks are of two kinds; first, crystalline rocks containing no fossils, and, second, crystalline rocks with fossils present. Aqueous rocks, on the other hand, are divided into primary, the oldest of its kind, secondary, tertiary, and quaternary. Add to these six strata, the top layer of soil, and the seven-fold testimony of geology is complete.

Physiology, too, has this same numeral seven, in marked prominence. The span of man's life is put by the Psalmist at "three score years and ten" (Ps. 90:10), that is, seventy years, or ten sevens. The varied phases of life itself Shakespeare puts at seven,—"One man in his time plays many parts, his acts being seven ages." Further, by the constant wearing away of its particles through activity, the whole body is said to change every seven years. In many of the diseases, too, common to mankind, the seventh, fourteenth, and twenty-first days are frequently of importance. In measles, for example, the rash appears about the fourteenth day, and the child is generally well again twenty-one days from the appearance of the rash. The period of quarantine for German measles is fourteen days, while for mumps it is twenty-one days. In chicken pox, the incubation period, when the disease is developing, is also fourteen days, and in whopping-cough it is put at seven to fourteen days. Why should not the number of days be varied, instead of seven prevailing?

Again, the workings of nature, as seen in the common bee, are most remarkable, and afford unique testimony to the fact of numerical plan in the works of God. The bee itself is composed of three parts, head, thorax, and abdomen. The thorax and abdomen are made up of ringed segments, generally three in the thorax, and nine in the abdomen. The legs of the insect are six in number. According to Arthur Mee, the well-known editor, the cells of the comb are from sixty to eighty thousand in number, and to put an egg in each, the Queen Bee lays some three thousand eggs per day. Fastened to the bottom of the cell, the egg remains for three days, when the larva, or grub, appears out of it. For six days it is fed by the nursing bees, and then, during the next thirty-six hours, the little grub spins itself into a robe of silk, a cocoon, within its cell. In other three days, a great change takes place. Wings and legs grow to full size, and the creature gnaws its way through, and emerges a working bee. Again, each hive contains from three to nine "royal princesses," soon to become queens. One day, the old queen leaves for a new hive, and is accompanied by two-thirds of the bees, the remaining one-third continuing the work of the old hive. Was it chance, or purpose, that brought about such a sequence of the numeral three? Surely here is evidence of arithmetical design, speaking of the Divine mind and plan behind all.

In Bible chronology, the same arithmetical law prevails. That given by God to Israel was based upon the numeral seven. On the seventh day they rested, in the seventh month were special feasts, in the seventh year the land lay fallow, while the forty-ninth—seven times seven—was the glorious emancipation year, the year of Jubilee.

A last, but most convincing, tribute to this mathematical arrangement in the works of God is paid by the vegetable kingdom. This the botanist divides into plants which he terms Monocotyledons, and those which he calls Dicotyledons. In a flower, the outer covering, or calyx, is made up of little leaves called sepals; while the inner cup, the corolla, is composed of the petals. In the center rise slender stalks, called stamens, in the middle of which is the pistil, consisting of the ovary and the stigma. The ovary contains seed-vessels, or carpels. In most Dicotyledons, the parts of the flower, sepals, petals, and stamens, are in sets of five or multiples of five, while in most Monocotyledons they are in threes or multiples of three. To this first class belongs the common sweet pea. Examine it, and you will find it has five sepals, five petals, and ten, or five + five, stamens. On the other hand, the narcissus is of the second class. It has three sepals, and three petals, which enclose the corola. In the latter there are three stamens visible from the top of the flower, and three farther down. There are three carpels making up the pistil, while in the ovary there are three cells.

Again the question arises, whence this marvelous symmetry and arrangement of numbers? That it pervades nature is plain. To use the words of Dr. A. T. Pierson: "A mathematical mind is manifest in the universe, in the planetary and stellar worlds, their distances and dimensions, densities, proportions, orbits, and periods of revolution. In the most minute as in the most majestic objects in nature the same laws govern. In the mineral realm, crystallization shows its squares, triangles, circles and polygons—cubes, cylinders, and pyramids or cones, all with exact angles and perfection of proportion. The million snowflakes have a million exquisite forms, each, under the microscope, revealing indescribable complexity and beauty."

God being, then, a God of perfect precision and order, expressed in terms of arithmetical law in all His works, it is but reasonable to expect a like expression in His Word. Such is the conclusion stated thus by F. W. Grant: "All natural sciences are ranging themselves under arithmetical law. Every law of nature, says Herschel, tends to express itself in terms of arithmetic. While astronomy preaches it to you from the starry spheres, the plants in the arrangement of their leaves and the division of their flowers, the animal kingdom shows its partiality among its different tribes for different numbers, the crystal talks mathematics to you from the window-pane. Why should not a law of number pervade Scripture also, and link God's Work and God's Word together,—or show His Word also to be His Work!"

For just as His Way is declared to be perfect (Ps. 18:30), so is His Word,—"The Law of the Lord is perfect" (Ps. 19:7).

4

Design in God's Word

"How can you reconcile the doctrine of the Trinity with reason?" said a young man to Daniel Webster. The silver-tongued American statesman, man of giant intellect, replied: "Do you expect to understand the arithmetic of Heaven?" The arithmetic of Heaven, like the things which God hath prepared for them that love Him, is outwith the natural comprehension of man; but, like those same things, "God hath revealed them unto us by His Spirit" (1 Cor. 2:10). Something of it the eye of faith can read in God's works, as it scans the perfection of order that characterizes them. It is, therefore, no matter for surprise to find this same order prevailing in His Word, for, like His Works, it, too, is marked by beauty of structure and design, woven into one complete pattern, which stretches from Genesis to the Revelation. So complete and comprehensive is this design as to embrace within it the simple numerals employed in the narrative. "There is unquestionable evidence of a numerical proportion and symmetry in this marvelous Book. Numbers and mathematical proportion mark it as a whole, and appear in its individual parts, with such frequency, and in such definite relations and conditions, as to evince a mathematical mind" (Dr. A. T. Pierson).

Numbers, therefore, in the Scriptures, not only bear their usual arithmetical value, but so harmonize with the general scheme as to convey each its own spiritual meaning. In ancient times, it is true, numbers were employed by the philosophers in the most grotesque and fantastic ways, being worked by them into speculations as useless as they were foolish. This, however, by no means discredits the idea of a prevailing numerical scheme in the Scriptures. The critic would have us to believe that these heathen uses of number, along with much of heathen mythology, provided the original from which much of the Bible was built up. The truth is not that the Scriptures are a development from these old-world legends, but that many of these are corruptions of the truth of the Scriptures. That many of them enshrine some seedling of truth goes to show, as the Word of God itself teaches (Rom. 1:19, 20), that, here and there, rays of Divine truth, scattered and dim, but none the less real, had burst through the gross darkness of heathendom.

Moreover, that numbers should bear a spiritual significance is entirely consistent, when it is remembered that the Old Testament Scriptures are largely typical in character. The all-embracing wisdom and power of God have combined to bring it about that while these writings are records of actual events, these very events are at the same time pictures, or types, of spiritual things. "The Great Architect and Builder had before Him the finished Temple of

Truth, before the first stone was laid." For example, in Genesis, chapter 1, we hear God break the awful silence with words empowered to illumine the chaotic darkness, saying: "Let there be light" (v. 3). The Holy Spirit, through Paul, records that event as a picture, or figure, of His Own work in the benighted souls of men, bringing them into the light of the Gospel, saying: "God who commanded the light to shine out of darkness hath shined in our hearts" (2 Cor. 4:6). Again, that re-creative work of God, as described in the same chapter, is used to depict the renewing work of the grace of God in salvation, for "if any man be in Christ, he is a new creature" (2 Cor. 5:17). In another place, writing to the Galatian believers, the great Apostle, contrasting the bondage that is of the law, with the liberty that is of grace, recalls the story of Hagar and Ishmael, explaining its meaning thus: "Which things are an allegory" (or type) (Gal. 4:24). The Word of God, then, is a book of spiritual significance, of perfect order and design.

Each book of the Bible, besides being the account of certain happenings, has its own peculiar purpose. Each is the illustration of some one important truth. Not only so, but these are set forth in such a way, that each follows the other in order of development. Were the sun to rise suddenly into the overhead sky, his rays would blind, not light us. But an all-wise Creator ordained that the dawn should be a gradual process, with little light increasing to much. So it is with the teaching of the various books of Scripture, which are graded to form a progression of truth, just in the order in which we are able to apprehend it.

The book of Genesis is the account of man, and of all that springs from him. The various forms of life, which have their origin in the first man, Adam, are there set forth. But all that pertains to Adam bears the taint of his sin, hence the absolute necessity of redemption. This is displayed in the book of Exodus, when a redeemed people go out from the bondage of Egypt on the ground of the shedding of blood. Redeemed people, however, need access into the presence of the Lord, must be taught the way into the sanctuary. This is the import of the book of Leviticus. Moreover, as those redeemed by blood, we take our place as pilgrims from the scene of bondage through the world-wilderness, our hopes set upon another land, the eye of the soul seeing a city which is invisible. But there are trials by the way, disappointments sometimes, and seeming defeats, from all of which God has many useful lessons He would have His people to learn. This is the experience of the book of Numbers. Again, the people of God, reaching Kadesh-Barnea, near to the land of promise, shrink back from entering into their possessions. Reaching it for a second time some thirty-eight years later, they now desire fully to enjoy the land God has given them. For the accomplishment of this, there are laws which must be observed, hence the book of Deuteronomy. Having attained to this experience, learning, as ever, by the things they suffer, they go on to know practically resurrection life, to wrestle against principalities and powers, and to be victorious as they follow their blessed Leader, the Man with the drawn sword, who ever precedes them. This is the book of Joshua. The various books of the Holy Scriptures, then, besides recounting actual happenings, convey spiritual truth set forth in progressive order, thus witnessing to precision and plan in the inspired Word.

This beauty of order is evident, too, within the book of Genesis itself. In chapter one, the great work of God upon this earth, preparing it as a home for His creature, is revealed in its seven stages. As the narrative proceeds, seven outstanding men pass before our view. These, in turn, are representative of a seven-fold experience that comprises the life of a believer: (1) Adam, the first man, typifies human nature as it is. His is the life of sin. (2) Next comes Abel, who is hated and opposed by Cain, picture of the strife between the Spirit and the flesh. Abel's is the life of struggle. (3) We next are introduced to Noah, who, safe within the Ark, passes through the waters of judgment into a new world. His is the life of salvation. (4) Abraham now comes before us, "the friend of God," the man who believes God, and goes out from his own land, at God's behest, not knowing whither he goes. His is the life of faith. (5) Next we see Isaac, who, in perfect obedience, accompanies his father to the altar on Mount Moriah. His is the life of sonship. (6) We now follow the fortunes of Jacob, serving his uncle diligently in Padan-aram. His is the life of service. (7) Finally, we see Joseph, the rejected outcast, slandered and suffering, at last honored, exalted, and reigning. His is the life of suffering, with glory to follow. Here again the order is progressive, and true to individual experience. To begin with, we were by nature in the state of sin, then followed the struggle, ending in the thrice-blessed experience of regeneration. This calls us to a walk of faith, which in turn brings the realization of sonship. To apprehend our sonship is to be truly ready for service, which will entail suffering, but will end in glory. Thus in those seven men shine forth seven colors, "the various shades of the true light of life, seen through the triangular prism of human nature, from the red of Adam, to the regal purple of Joseph."

The presence of design has been pointed out in the book of Psalms, where an interesting correspondence is found, between the five sections of the Psalms and the five books of Moses composing the Pentateuch. In the Psalms, the first section, Psalms 1 to 41, ending with the words "Amen and amen," corresponds to the book of Genesis, the book of creation, as seen in Psalm 8 verse 3: "When I consider Thy heavens, the work of Thy fingers, the moon and the stars which Thou hast ordained." The second division, Psalms 42 to 72, ending as in Section 1, corresponds to Exodus, with redemption for its theme, as in Psalm 51:1: "Have mercy upon me, O God, according to Thy lovingkindness: according unto the multitude of Thy tender mercies, blot out my transgressions." Section 3 finds its corresponding book in Leviticus, the book of the Sanctuary. It comprises Psalms 73 to 89, ends also as in Section 1, and has for its leading theme the thought of Psalm 84:1: "How amiable are Thy tabernacles, O Lord of Hosts! My soul longeth, yea, even fainteth for the courts of the Lord."

The fourth division, Psalms 90 to 106, ends with the word "Amen," and is the parallel division to Numbers, the wilderness book. Hence Psalm 90:9: "We spend our years as a tale that is told." In the last division, Psalms 107 to 150, the closing words are "Praise ye the Lord," the corresponding book is Deuteronomy, and the theme obedience, as in Psalm 119:1: "Blessed are the undefiled in the way, who walk in the law of the Lord." This same systematic presentation of truth holds, too, in the New Testament. In the Gospels, we have the revelation of the worth and work of the Person of Christ, the Head of the Church. In the Acts and the Epistles, we deal with the Church, "which is His Body," and find instruction as to how members of that Body ought to walk. Finally, in the Revelation, we have the glorious final and eternal union of Head and Body.

But the presence, in the Word of God, of definite plan and order is evident not only in general fashion throughout, but in detail in the very numbers employed in it, and to begin with is written large over the whole Book in the nature of its composition. The following extract from a Canadian magazine, quoted by Walter Scott, is of interest: "The books of the Old Testament are 36 in number (counting Samuel, Kings, and Chronicles as one book each, as is really the fact). The simplest division of 36 is into 3 by 12. Put this number into the symbolism of these figures, and what do we find? Three (3) is the Divine and 12 the governmental number; taken together, they give you 'God in government.' What more precise definition could we have of the books of the Law? But the books of the New Testament are 27 in number. And this is the cube of 3; it is 3 times 3 times 3;

the most absolutely perfect number there can
be, the only one into which none but the symbol
of Divine fullness enters or can enter. Thus it is
God and only God,—God in His Own absolute
perfection,—revealed in the New Testament
pages,—in the Gospel of His grace." The Bible
as a whole has 63 books on this same reckoning,
and 63=7 x 9, or 7 x 3 x 3. Seven (7) is the
symbol of perfection, 3 of divine manifestation;
3 times 3, that manifestation intensified. Hence
the numerical significance of the books of the
Bible is, "God glorified in His perfectly
accomplished work."

Taking a survey of the whole Book, further
evidence of design is to be seen in the symmetry
of its very books. First come five books of
history, Genesis to Deuteronomy, and following
this, twelve books of minor prophecy, including
Joshua to Esther. Then follow five poetical
books, Job to the Song of Solomon; next, five
books of major prophecy, Isaiah to Daniel; and
last, twelve books of minor prophecy, Hosea to
Malachi. This gives a series of 5, 12, 5, 5, and 12.
Further, in the New Testament, we have to begin
with five historical books, Matthew to Acts; then
twenty-one, or three times seven Epistles,
Romans to Jude; and, finally, the book of the
Revelation to complete the structure. Leaving
the Book as a whole, we notice numerical plan
in some of its component parts, notably in Psalm
119. The Psalm consists of 22 sections, each of 8
verses. Each section corresponds to a letter of
the Hebrew alphabet, which letters head their
respective sections. A similar numerical
arrangement is evident, also, in the book of
Lamentations, which consists of 5 laments

corresponding to the 5 chapters. Of these, the first two and the last two each contain 22 verses, while the middle chapter contains 66 verses, or 3 times 22.

Thus is displayed, in a variety of forms, the presence, in the Word of God, of definite numerical design. One has well expressed it in these words: "Its almost mathematical precision, easily to be discerned substantially by the most unspiritual, challenges the infidel to account for what he cannot conceive to have been done by the contrivance and connivance of man. Here is a simple, easy problem, which is as open to the unlearned as to the learned—to all classes at once. Yet, settle it as it must be settled, you are brought face to face with God. It is the finger of God. This simple enumeration, this babe's arithmetic, is a web that Goliath's sword can never pierce, and whose meshes will hold powerless the stoutest champions of unbelief. Try it, gentlemen! Learn how God has mocked all your philosophy with the mere enumeration of 1, 2, 3!" (F. W. Grant).

5

The Numeral One

Since the number "one" is not composed of other numbers, but is independent of all others, it excludes all difference. Moreover, it is the source of all others, and so marks the beginning. As excluding difference, it denotes Divine unity, supremacy, and independency, speaking of a "sufficiency which needs no other, and an independency which admits no other." As being the source of all others, it denotes origin.

The first book of the Bible, Genesis, deals with the beginnings of things,—"In the beginning God" (Gen. 1:1). In it God is displayed in sovereignty and in supremacy, as the Giver and Sustainer of life in all its forms. Two words are made use of in the Old Testament Scriptures for "one"; *yacheed*, which signifies "only one," and *echad*, meaning "one of others." An example of the use of the former is found in Genesis 22:2: "Take now thy son, thine only son Isaac, whom thou lovest." The latter is used in Genesis 2:24, relating to the union of two persons: "Therefore shall a man leave his father and mother, and shall cleave unto his wife; and they shall be one flesh." But *yacheed* is never used of God. Always the word is *echad*, one of others, signifying not an absolute unity, but a compound unity, three in one and one in three, the glorious Trinity. This same word *echad* is found in Deuteronomy 6:4: "The Lord our God is one Lord." Again, in Zechariah 14:9, speaking of the coming rule of the Prince of Peace, these words occur: "And the Lord shall be King over all the earth; in that day shall there be one Lord, and His Name one."

In 1 Kings 6, a description is given of Solomon's wonderful temple, with its two cherubim "within the oracle." In verse 25 this is stated: "Both the cherubim were of one measure and one size," speaking of the unity of the governmental attributes of Jehovah. In 2 Chronicles is recorded the defiance by King Hezekiah of Sennacherib of Assyria. Coming to the throne when the land was given over to idolatry, Hezekiah removed the groves, and cast down the idols, so that Sennacherib could say of him: "Hath not the same Hezekiah taken away his high places, and his altars, and commanded Judah and Jerusalem, saying, 'Ye shall worship before one altar and burn incense upon it'" (32:12). Here again the numeral "one" is emphatic, declaring the unity of worship. Again, Paul, in that masterly oration to the philosophizing Greeks on Mars Hill (Acts 17), gives another example of the significance of this number. In verse 26, he leads his hearers to the thought that, far from being an image produced by man, God was the Creator of man, and in this sense man is His offspring: "[God] hath made of one blood all nations of men." One here marks the unity of the race.

The first recorded words of the Lord Jesus

are found in Psalm 40:7, 8. Taken by the writer into the secrets of a past eternity, we hear Him say: "Lo, I come: in the volume of the Book it is written of Me, I delight to do Thy will, O My God; yea, Thy law is within My heart." This first saying marks the unity of purpose of the Son of God, perfect obedience to the Father. Moreover, in the one recorded saying of Jesus during His first twenty-nine years among men, this same unity of purpose is still with Him: "Wist ye not that I must be about My Father's business?" (Luke 2:49). Again, the first recorded words after He entered upon His public ministry are not without significance in these days. Repelling the attacks of Satan in the wilderness, He said with three-fold emphasis: "It is written" (Luke 4), thus leading us back to the Scriptures, as the origin and source of all power against the wiles of the tempter. In Hebrews 9, the unity of Christ's one Sacrifice of Himself is brought out. In verse 7, the High Priest went into the Holiest of all "once every year"; in verse 11, Christ, "the High Priest of good things to come," entered in once into the Holy Place, having obtained eternal redemption for us; in verse 26, "Once, in the end of the age, hath He appeared to put away sin by the sacrifice of Himself." The purpose which the Son of God had set before Him, He carried to fullest fruition, with blessed results both to God and to man. Hence in Ephesians 4:4-6 is found the unity of the Church, His Body, which He purchased with His own blood: "There is one body, and one spirit, even as ye are called in one hope of your calling; one Lord, one faith, one baptism, one God and Father of all, who is above all, and through all, and in you all." In spite, therefore, of apparent confusion amongst the people of God, here is a seven-fold affirmation of its real and abiding unity, the more so because in the center of all is the "one Lord."

Words that occur only once in the Holy Scriptures demand our special attention. There are three such words, worthy of our interest because they all refer to the Scriptures themselves. The first is found in Hebrews 4:12, where we are told that the Word of God is "a discerner [or critic] of the thoughts and intents of the heart." It is as though God, foreseeing a day when men would presume to install themselves in the office of critic of His own Word, had forestalled them by reserving that name and office for that very Word itself.

A second word occurs in 2 Corinthians 2:17, where the Apostle writes: "We are not as many, which corrupt the Word of God." The word here used is derived from another, meaning "to eat quickly." This meaning easily became changed to "the place where eating is done," that is, a tavern. In course of time, it came to mean "the keeper of a tavern," and, from a practice only too common amongst them, ultimately meant "to water down," or "to adulterate." Here the Apostle condemns the practice of many to-day, who would seek to corrupt, "to water down," the Word of God.

The third word is used by Paul in 2 Corinthians 4:1, 2: "Therefore, seeing we have this ministry, as we have received mercy, we faint not; but have renounced the hidden things of dishonesty, not walking in craftiness, nor handling the Word of God deceitfully." This word, to "handle deceitfully," comes from a word meaning "a slave." Later, it came to mean "to make a slave of anyone." This was effected by trickery, by some ruse. Hence the word became more debased in meaning, and signified any cunning method of catching by deceit. Thus with three most significant words, each occurring once only, does God warn against the unscrupulous use of His Holy Word.

6

The Numeral Two

If the numeral one denotes unity, denying the possibility of difference, two affirms that there is a difference, there is another. This difference may oppose and be for evil, or it may confirm and be for good. Speaking of division, it is symbolical of evil; speaking of addition it represents confirmation. Generally, then, two speaks of fullness of testimony, either for good or for evil.

In John 8, the Lord Jesus Christ, in answer to the challenge of the Pharisees, said: "It is also written in your law, that the testimony of two men is true. I am One that bear witness of Myself, and the Father that sent Me beareth witness of Me" (vv. 17-18). Here was two-fold testimony to His Divine mission. Moreover, in two Testaments, the Old Covenant and the New, is contained the complete testimony of God's attitude towards men. Again, while the first sentence in the Scriptures is a statement of God's perfect creation,—"In the beginning God created the heaven and the earth" (Gen. 1:1), the second speaks of ruin, from some unknown, but evil, cause,—"And the earth was without form and a void; and darkness was upon the face of the deep" (Gen. 1:2). The second thing brought into being, as recorded in that same chapter, was light, and immediately thereafter mention is made of division: "God saw the light that it was good; and God divided the light from the darkness" (v. 4).

The work of the second day was also marked by this thought of division. "God said, 'Let there be a firmament in the midst of the waters, and let it divide the waters from the waters'" (v. 6). Of the seven representative men of Genesis, the second was Abel, who was characterized by his difference from Cain, his brother. In the same book, when two men are found coupled together, it is with a view to marking the difference between them, as with Abraham and Lot, Isaac and Ishmael, Jacob and Esau.

Again, in the construction of the Tabernacle (Ex. 26), two materials were of frequent use, gold and shittim-wood, testimony to the two-fold nature of Jesus Christ, gold signifying His Divinity, shittim-wood His Humanity. The ten commandments, too, God's Covenant with Israel, were contained on two tables of stone, "tables of testimony" (Ex. 31:18), the expression of God's demand of righteousness from man. Also, when an Israelite had committed certain offenses, he was enjoined to confess his sin, and for his trespass bring "two turtle-doves, or two young pigeons, unto the Lord; one for a sin-offering, and the other for a burnt-offering" (Lev. 5:7). Similarly, when the leper was healed, the priest was commanded to take two birds (Lev. 14:4), while in Lev. 16 two goats were taken. Thus did Jehovah offer testimony to the completeness of the work of atonement. Close to the borders of the land of promise, Israel sent out spies to confirm that which needs no confirmation, the Word of God, and of these, two men bore testimony to the truth.

Later, in the erection of the Temple, Solomon brought a skilled worker in brass, Hiram of Tyre, who raised two pillars of brass (1 Kings 7:15), testimony to the enduring character of the millennial glory, when a King greater than Solomon shall reign in righteousness. When that kingdom of Solomon's became divided, Jeroboam, trying to consolidate his position by preventing the people from going to worship at Jerusalem, erected two calves of gold (1 Kings 12:28), complete testimony to the idolatry of God's people. Then followed the witness of two prophets, Elijah and Elisha (2 Kings 2), full testimony of God against the idolatrous nation.

The significance of the numeral two, as denoting enmity, is seen in an instructive way in the Psalms. Of the five divisions of the whole book referred to in Chapter 4 the second Psalm in each contains this thought. (1) Psalm 2 depicts the rulers of the earth taking counsel together against the Lord's Anointed, and foretells His final and complete triumph over His enemies. (2) Psalm 43:2 asks this question: "Why go I mourning because of the oppression of the enemy?" And again, in verse 5, asks: "Why art thou cast down, O my soul? And why art thou disquieted within me?" (3) In Psalm 74 the desolations wrought by the enemy are spoken of, and then the question is asked: "O God, how long shall the adversary reproach? Shall the enemy blaspheme Thy Name for ever?" (v. 10). (4) Turning to Psalm 91, we find the place of security from the enemy: "He is my refuge and my fortress: my God; in Him will I trust" (v. 2); and the doom of the enemy is foretold: "Only with thine eyes shalt thou behold and see the reward of the wicked" (v. 8). (5) Lastly, in Psalm 108, the theme is the mercy of the Lord, who helps His people from trouble, and accomplishes complete deliverance: "Through God we shall do valiantly: for He it is that shall tread down our enemies" (v. 13).

As in the Old Testament, so in the New Testament Scriptures, this numeral two, symbol of testimony, is prominent. In the two blind men of Matthew 9:27 is found a testimony to the moral blindness of Israel, over whose heart unbelief had drawn a veil, that they should not see in the Lord Jesus their promised Hope. In chapter 22 of Matthew's Gospel, Christ declared that the whole law, God's testimony to man, hung on two commandments: "On these two commandments hang all the law and the prophets" (v. 40). Moreover, wherever two epistles are given, the second one has special reference to the enemy.

In 2 Corinthians, Paul speaks of the power of the enemy, the working of Satan. In chapter 1 he refers to tribulation and sufferings, to being "pressed out of measure, above strength, insomuch that we despaired even of life" (vv. 4-8). In chapter 2 we hear him tell of heaviness (v. 1), of being sorry (v. 3), of "much affliction and anguish" (v. 4), and of "Satan getting an advantage over us" (v. 11). In chapter 12 he speaks of "the messenger of Satan to buffet" him (v. 7).

Again, in 2 Thessalonians, the Apostle warns

them of the apostasy, now rapidly settling around us, and of the revelation of "that man of sin, the son of perdition" (2:3). Writing to Timothy, in his second letter, Paul describes the confusion of the visible Church, with false teachers "overthrowing the faith of some" (2:18). In 3:5, he tells of men having "a form of godliness, but denying the power thereof." In 4:3, men refuse sound doctrine, and "heap to themselves teachers, having itching ears."

Turning to Peter's Epistles, we have, in the second one, apostasy foretold, with false teachers "denying the Lord that bought them" (2:1); while in chapter 3 he tells of the "scoffers who would come in the last days" (3:3).

Finally, in 2 John 7, we read: "Many deceivers are entered into the world, who confess not that Jesus Christ is come in the flesh. This is a deceiver, and an antichrist."

The numeral two, as indicative of testimony, has several interesting applications to the Lord Jesus Christ Himself. He is the second Person of the Godhead. He is the Word of God, the expression or testimony of God. In 1 Corinthians 15:47, He is spoken of as "the second Man," while in Revelation 3:14, He is the "faithful and true Witness." In His own Person was a two-fold nature, for He was perfect God and perfect Man. In His life and death He bore a double testimony, declaring man's guilt and revealing God's grace. When men took Him, and with wicked hands crucified and slew Him, they testified to their hatred and contempt by putting him between two thieves. The Roman soldier who plunged the spear into His side drew forth blood and water (Jn. 19:34), a two-fold testimony to the efficacy of His death, one for sin's expiation, the other for its purification. Finally, in the coming days of tribulation, there will still be two witnesses, bearing full testimony to Christ in His royal and priestly rights (Rev. 11:3).

7

The Numeral Three

There are in measurement three dimensions, length, breadth, and thickness. These go to make up a solid, and therefore three speaks of solidity. It is the symbol of completeness This solidity and completeness suggest the Triune God, hence three denotes Divine testimony or manifestation. This manifestation is sometimes in resurrection of things moral, physical, and spiritual. Accordingly, three, while denoting Divine manifestation, or Divine perfection, is also the symbol of resurrection. Next to seven, it is the most commonly used number in Scripture.

There are three great all-embracing attributes of God, omniscience, omnipotence, and omnipresence. The whole cycle of time is complete in three divisions, past, present, and future. Three capabilities include every activity of man, thought, word, and deed. On the third day of the works of God recorded in Genesis 1 the dry land emerged from the waters, figure of Christ in resurrection. The Sanctuary, God's dwelling-place, a perfect cube in shape, was the highest place of worship. In Genesis 18:1, this statement concerning Abraham is found: "Jehovah appeared unto him in the plains of

Mamre." Verse 2 tells that when Abraham lifted up his eyes he saw three men. Verse 9 has these words: "And they said unto him;" while verse 17 begins: "And the Lord said." Again, although addressing three men, verse 3 records that Abraham three times addressed them in the singular: "If now I have found favor in thy sight, pass not away, I pray thee, from thy servant." Evidently, this manifestation of God was in a three-fold form. Again, Abraham is three times described as the friend of God (2 Chron. 20:7; Is. 41:8; Jas. 2:23).

In Numbers 6:24-26 is found the three-fold blessing given by God to Aaron, with which he was to bless the people: "The Lord bless thee and keep thee; the Lord make His face shine upon thee and be gracious unto thee; the Lord lift up His countenance upon thee and give thee peace." Here is divine perfection of blessing. In Deuteronomy 17:15, 18:5, and 18:15, we have Christ in all the perfection of His offices for His people. In the first passage He is King: "One from among thy brethren shalt thou set King over thee." In the second passage He appears as Priest: "The Lord thy God hath chosen Him out of all thy tribes, to stand to minister in the name of the Lord." In the last, He is shown as Prophet: "The Lord thy God will raise up unto thee a Prophet, from the midst of thee, of thy brethren, like unto me." In Isaiah 6:3, the seraphim declared the perfect holiness of God, crying, "Holy, holy, holy is the Lord of Hosts." Also, when at the instigation of envious princes, King Darius forbade by edict the making of request of any save himself for thirty days, Daniel continued to manifest his belief in God, for "he kneeled upon his knees three times a day, and prayed, and gave thanks before his God, as he did aforetime" (Dan. 6:10).

Again, during three years of public life, the Lord Himself was seeking in vain for fruit from Israel, and was completing the manifestation of that nation's failure. At the outset of that ministry, He brought men back to the Word of God in all its perfection of supply against temptation, in a thrice-repeated "It is written," quoted from the Book of Deuteronomy (Luke 4). During that ministry, moreover, a three-fold testimony from Heaven was the complete manifestation of God's pleasure with His Son. First, at the Jordan, a voice from Heaven was heard, saying: "This is my beloved Son, in whom I am well pleased" (Matt. 3:17). Then, on the mountain, when the Lord Jesus was transfigured in the presence of His three disciples, again a voice spoke from the cloud: "This is My beloved Son: hear Him" (Luke 9:35). Later, when His hour was almost come, He prayed, saying, "Father, glorify Thy Name." Then was heard a voice from Heaven, saying, "I have both glorified it, and will glorify it again" (Jn. 12:28). Three times, too, He displayed His supreme power over death, in that He raised three persons, Jairus' daughter, the son of a widow of the town of Nain, and Lazarus. Again, when the Pharisees came seeking a sign, Christ referred them to the manifestation of God through the prophet Jonah, "three days and three nights in the whale's belly" (Matt. 12:40). At His trial, the failure of the best resolves of man was fully shown in Peter's three-fold denial (Mark 14:72), while the third hour, the crucifixion hour, was the manifestation of the powers of darkness. For three hours, too, from the sixth to the ninth hour, darkness enveloped Him, while the holiness of God manifested itself in relation to His Son made sin for us. The superscription over the Cross, written in three languages, testified to the completeness of His rejection by man (Luke 23:38).

The third day, however, manifested God's entire satisfaction with the work of His Son, Jesus Christ, for on that day He rose again according to the Scriptures (1 Cor. 15:4). Moreover, the divine completeness of His shepherd-care is brought out in that He is declared to be the Good Shepherd in His death (Jn. 10:11), the Great Shepherd in His resurrection (Heb. 13:20), and the Chief Shepherd at His coming again (1 Pet. 5:4). And last, the Lord's commission to His disciples, as given in Matthew 28:19, is a three-fold and full manifestation of the Godhead: "Go ye, therefore, and teach all nations, baptizing them in the name of the Father, and of the Son, and of the Holy Spirit."

Again, three appearings, as recorded in Hebrews 9, will complete His work: "Once in the end of the age hath He appeared to put away sin by the Sacrifice of Himself" (v. 26) tells of the foundation laid. "Christ is not entered into the holy places made with hands, the figures of the true; but into Heaven itself, there to appear in the presence of God for us" (v. 24), speaks of the work continued. "Unto them that look for Him shall He appear the second time, without sin, unto salvation" (v. 28), will lay the top stone on the completed structure. Peter, about the sixth hour went on to the house-top in Joppa to pray, and beheld a vision, which "was done thrice" (Acts 10:16). Three times is the word "fullness" employed; the fullness of God (Eph. 3:19), the fullness of Christ (Eph. 4:13), and the fullness of the Godhead (Col. 2:9). Three times, too, are believers on the Lord Jesus Christ called to "walk worthy" of Him: (1) "I beseech you that ye walk worthy of the vocation wherewith ye are called" (Eph. 4:1); (2) "That ye might walk worthy of the Lord unto all pleasing" (Col. 1:10); and (3) "That ye would walk worthy of God, who hath called you unto His kingdom and glory" (1 Thess. 2:12).

The complete manifestation of evil is seen in the three-fold enemy of the believer—the world, the flesh, and the Devil,—while the completeness of temptation is recorded in 1 John 2:16: "The lust of the flesh, and the lust of the eyes, and the pride of life." In this same epistle, the divinely perfect witness to the grace of God on earth is given: "There are three that bear witness on earth, the Spirit, and the water, and the blood" (5:8). The completeness of the apostasy of men is summed up in Jude 11: "Woe unto them! for they have gone in the way of Cain, and ran greedily after the error of Balaam for reward, and perished in the gainsaying of Core."

Lastly, the final City, the manifestation of the glory of God, is a perfect cube, "the length, and the breadth, and the height of it are equal" (Rev. 21:16).

8

The Numeral Four

The number four, composed of three + one, denotes that which follows the manifestation of God in the Trinity, that is, His creative work. It is the number of the corners of the earth, and so speaks of earthly completeness and universality. Being the first of the numerals admitting of simple division, it marks, too, weakness. Four, then, is symbolic of universality, of creation, of man in his relation to the universe, and, because of man's failure towards God, of weakness.

Accordingly, four Gospels contain the declaration of God's love to the world in the gift of His Son, a love acting with this universal purpose, "that whosoever believeth in Him should not perish" (Jn. 3:16). The fourth book of the Bible, too, the book of Numbers, is the book of the wilderness journey of the believer through this world, as is also the fourth division of the Psalms. On the fourth day, the material creation was completed, the fifth and sixth days being occupied with the furnishing and peopling of the earth (Gen. 1:14-19). In Genesis 2 a river is spoken of, which, going out of Eden, branched into four parts, and fertilized the earth (v. 10). Again, in Genesis 10, is given a four-fold description of mankind, the descendants of Noah and his sons: "By these were the isles of the Gentiles divided in their lands; every one after his tongue, after their families, in their nations" (v. 5). The dream of Nebuchadnezzar, as revealed by the prophet Daniel (Dan. 2:31-36), foretold four great world-powers; and again in chapter 7 the record of Daniel's vision speaks of four beasts, symbols of the Gentile empires, with sovereignty over all the earth. Again, in Ezekiel, we read of four living creatures, each with four faces, and every one having four wings, with hands of a man under their wings on their four sides (1:5-8). In 7:2, the four corners of the land are spoken of, while in 10:9, we have four wheels; in 14:21, four sore judgments; in 37:9, four winds; in 40:41, four tables; and in 45:19, four corners of the altar.

In Zechariah 1:18-21 there are four horns and four carpenters; while in 6:1 there are four chariots. The parable of the sower, as recorded in Matthew 13, speaks of four kinds of soil upon the world-field. Four views of the Heavenly Jerusalem are given in Revelation 21, just as in Ezekiel 48 are found four views of the earthly Jerusalem. The book of the Revelation, too, with its universal judgments, tells of four angels, four winds of the earth, and four corners of the earth (7:1); of four living creatures (4:8), and of the four quarters of the earth (20:8).

9

The Numeral Five

The number five is composed of four + one. We have seen that four speaks of man in his relation to what is created, while one speaks of the all-sufficient God. Five, then, denotes man as responsible under the government of God. As four speaks of the works of God in creation, so five declares His works in redemption, and so is symbolic of grace. But grace is favor shown to the unworthy, and therefore five speaks of unworthiness or weakness. Five, then, is the number of exercise and responsibility, of weakness, and of grace in spite of weakness.

There are five books of Moses, the books connected specially with man, his failure and God's remedy. When the Israelites, redeemed by blood, quitted the land of Egypt, they did so in a formation that spoke of weakness, and consequent grace, "by five in a rank" (Ex. 13:18, margin).

Forty years later, after many days of learning the ways of God in the wilderness, they reached the banks of the Jordan, and again in symbol declared that it was all of grace that they entered the land, for they went "marshaled by five" (Josh. 1:14, margin). In Exodus 30 is described the holy anointing oil in its five-fold composition, speaking of pure grace: "Take thou also unto thee principal spices, of pure myrrh five hundred shekels, and of sweet cinnamon half so much, even two hundred and fifty shekels, and of cassia five hundred shekels after the shekel of the sanctuary, and of oil olive an hin" (vv. 23, 24).

Here are represented the moral graces and perfections of Christ as Son of Man, the chiefest among ten thousand, and the altogether lovely, in the energy of the Holy Spirit. Hence the oil must only contain the principal, or most excellent, of the spices. The first of these, myrrh, is a fragrant spice, of bitter taste but of sweet aroma. It flows freely from the tree, and so figures the grace of His lips, which "were like lilies, dropping sweet-smelling myrrh" (Cant. 5:13). The second, sweet cinnamon, is the inner bark, sweet and fragrant, speaking of the excellency of His character, as observed by those who were of the inner circle, and moved in His private life. The third, sweet calamus, forms the pith of the tree, type of the sweet perfection of Christ in His thoughts and affections. The last spice, cassia, is the outer bark, symbol of this same excellency of character, but manifested in His public walk before men. The olive oil denotes the Holy Spirit, in whose energy He continually acted. This was to be a full hin, for to His Son the Father "gave not the Spirit by measure."

Again, in the construction of the Tabernacle, five and its multiples prevail, for weakness can only worship through grace. The outer court was one hundred cubits long and fifty cubits wide. On either side were twenty pillars, while along each end were ten pillars, making sixty in all, that is, five times twelve, or grace in government. Further, the pillars upholding the curtains were five cubits apart and five high. The whole of the outer curtain, too, was divided into squares of twenty-five cubits. Also, the brazen altar was five by five cubits, while the building itself was ten cubits high, forty wide, and thirty long. In Leviticus 26:8, God's promise to His people, on condition of keeping His commandments and walking in His statutes, was that five of them would chase a hundred, that is, weakness clothed in the might of God. When the stripling, David, opposed and overthrew the giant of Gath, it was with "five smooth stones out of the brook" (1 Sam. 17:40), the insignificance of man supplemented by perfect grace. Five books of the Bible deal largely with the heart of man. These are the books known collectively as the Psalms, namely, Job, Psalms, Proverbs, Ecclesiastes, and Song of Solomon.

In the Gentile image of Daniel 2 five parts are mentioned, the fifth, the stone kingdom absorbing all others, being a rule in glory and in grace. In the parable of the Ten Virgins (Matt. 25), five of them were wise and five foolish. Again, in Luke 9, a multitude of about five thousand men were graciously fed by the Lord Jesus out of five loaves and two fishes, grace magnified in weakness (verses 13,14). Paul, writing to the Corinthians, expresses his desire to speak "five words with my understanding" (1 Cor. 14:19); that is, words uttered in weakness, depending on God to clothe them with power.

Finally, there is used in the New Testament,

five times over, the word "Parakleetos." Four times it is found in John's Gospel, applied to the Holy Spirit, the Comforter, and once it appears in John's first epistle, applied to the Lord Jesus Himself, the Advocate (1 Jn. 2:1). So is expressed the perfect grace of our God, meeting us His people in our helplessness, providing an Advocate within us for Him that we may not sin, and an Advocate in His presence for us if we do sin.

10

The Numeral Six

The numeral six is two times three. But two speaks of division or evil, and three of manifestation. Hence six denotes manifestation of evil. Again, six falls short of the numeral of perfection, seven, thus indicating incompleteness, and so is the symbol of man, without Christ.

On the sixth day, man was created, while six days were decreed for his labors. The descendants of Cain are given only to the sixth generation. In Genesis 22 the words "burnt offering" are mentioned six times, the seventh being reserved for the Divinely perfect Substitute (v. 8), the Lamb of God's providing. When the enraged Pharaoh pursued the Israelites, he did so with six hundred chosen chariots (Ex. 14:7), full expression of Satanic power. Later, when they had entered the land, God provided for their safety from the avenger of blood in the setting up of six cities, the seventh and perfect security being the Lord Jesus Himself (Jos. 20).

Solomon, in the days of his glorious kingdom, drew an annual revenue of six hundred and sixty-six talents of gold (1 Kings 10:14). When he made his great throne of ivory overlaid with gold, it had six steps (v. 19), for his glory fell short of perfection, and his kingdom was soon to be divided. In Proverbs 6:16 we read: "These six things doth the Lord hate." This is evil incompleted, for the next phrase says: "Yea, seven are an abomination unto Him." Of Gog's mighty host (Ezek. 39:2), God spared one-sixth part; that is, six parts composed the host, of which one part was spared in Divine sovereignty.

In John 2:6, when the Lord was about to perform that first miracle in Cana of Galilee, six waterpots of stone were set up, picture of man's failure to bring in blessing. Again, the hatred of man to God's Son found full declaration in that six times was the charge made against Him that He had a demon (Mark 3:22; Luke 11:15; John 7:20; 8:48; 8:52; and 10:20). Further, although Judge Pilate condemned Him to death, yet six persons united to testify Him innocent, Pilate himself (Luke 23:14), Herod (23:15), Judas (Matt. 27:4), Pilate's wife (Matt. 27:19), the dying thief (Luke 23:41), and the Centurion (Luke 23:47).

Moreover, as the Son of God hung between the malefactors, displaying God's limitless love and man's boundless enmity, about the sixth hour came a darkness upon the land (Matt. 27:45). In Revelation 13, verses 11-18, is the description of a being, who will effect great wonders, and rule with despotic power. Verse 18 says of him: "His number is Six hundred threescore and six," or 666.

Three men stand out pre-eminently in the Scriptures as the avowed enemy of God and His people, and each of these is branded with six, the number of man. First, in 1 Samuel 17:4-

7, we have Goliath, the giant of Gath, whose height was six cubits, and who wore six pieces of armor, his spearhead weighing six hundred shekels of iron. Second, in Daniel 3:1, is related how Nebuchadnezzar the king erected in the plain of Dura, in the province of Babylon, an image of gold, sixty cubits high and six cubits broad. Third, in Revelation 13, is the account of Antichrist, whose number is Six hundred and sixty-six. He is the trinity of human perfection, the perfection of imperfection, the culmination of human pride in independence of God and opposition to His Christ. The first, marked by 6, speaks of the pride of fleshly might; the second, by 66, denotes the pride of absolute dominion; while the third, marked by 666, symbolizes the pride of Satanic guidance.

11

The Numeral Seven

The numeral seven is composed of four + three, four speaking of the creature and three of Divine manifestation. Seven, therefore, represents the creature as manifesting the Creator. It is the symbol of spiritual perfection, either of good or of evil. It is the most frequent numeral in the Scriptures, being found over fifty times in the book of the Revelation, where things both good and evil come to a climax.

The Sabbath was the seventh day, when, after six days of work, God rested in the knowledge of its perfectness. Enoch, the seventh from Adam, "was not, for God took him." Moses, too, was the seventh from Abraham. In Genesis 12:2, 3, is given the seven-fold blessing pronounced by God upon Abraham: (1) "I will make of thee a great nation, (2) and I will bless thee, (3) and make thy name great, (4) and thou shalt be a blessing: (5) And I will bless them that bless thee (6) and curse him that curseth thee, (7) and in thee shall all families of the earth be blessed."

Again, to the people of Israel God gave a similar seven-fold promise, secured in its beginning and ending with the declaration, "I am the Lord." His words were these: (1) "I will bring you out from under the burdens of the Egyptians, (2) and I will rid you out of their bondage, (3) and I will redeem you with a stretched-out arm and with great judgments, (4) and I will take you to me for a people, (5) and I will be to you a God . . . (6) and I will bring you in unto the land concerning the which I did swear to give it to Abraham, to Isaac, and to Jacob; (7) and I will give it to you for an heritage" (Ex. 6:6-8). In this seven-fold "I will" is expressed the perfection of the purposes of Jehovah.

In Leviticus 14, where the law of the leper is stated, he was to be sprinkled seven times (v. 7). Also, there were seven Feasts of Jehovah, some of which lasted for seven days. Again, when Balak, the Moabite king, would have the hireling Balaam to curse Israel, he set up for him seven altars, and prepared seven bullocks and seven rams, the perfection of idolatrous worship (Num. 23:29). When the people of God encompassed Jericho, they were preceded by seven priests carrying seven trumpets of ram's horns, and on the seventh day at God's command encompassed it seven times. Then was displayed the completeness of the victory of faith, and of the destruction of the city of the curse (Josh. 6).

Further, in the book of Judges, seven weak things were used by God to confound the mighty, marking the spiritual perfection of God's works of deliverance. In 3:21, He made use of a left-handed man; in 3:31, of an ox-goad; in 4:4, of a woman; in 4:21, of a tent-peg; in 9:53, of a piece of millstone; in 7:20, of pitchers and trumpets; and in 15:15, of the jaw-bone of an ass.

In 1 Samuel 16:10 are the seven sons of Jesse, while in 2 Samuel 21:9 we have the seven sons of Saul. Matthew 12:45 speaks of seven more wicked spirits, the very acme of evil. In Matthew 18:22, the Lord Jesus Christ laid down the perfect measure of forgiveness, seventy times seven. In Mark 16:9, Mary Magdalene is spoken of, with this comment: "Out of whom He had cast seven demons," again the very climax of iniquity. In Acts 6:3, that the apostles might not need to "leave the Word of God and serve tables," seven men "of honest report, full of the Holy Spirit and wisdom," were chosen to manage the temporal affairs. In the same book it is recorded how God, fighting for His people Israel, destroyed seven nations in the land of Canaan (13:19).

Seven epistles were written to the churches, giving perfect instruction in all matters pertaining to life and godliness, while seven letters to the churches, in the Revelation, give the complete, inspired church history. In the same book are seven candlesticks, seven stars, seven lamps, seven angels, and seven spirits, while seven seals secure the book completely, and in seven last plagues is "filled up the wrath of God" (Rev. 15:1).

12

The Numeral Eight

This numeral consists of seven + one. We have seen that seven denotes perfection, and one beginning. Accordingly, eight is the symbol of a new beginning. It is associated with resurrection and regeneration, the beginning of a new order of things.

When the floods of the wrath of God swept the old world, "Noah, the eighth person, a preacher of righteousness" (2 Pet. 2:5), stepped from the ark into a new world, to begin the race, as it were, anew. In all eight persons were saved (1 Pet. 3:20). In Genesis 21:4, we read: "Abraham circumcised his son Isaac being eight days old, as God had commanded him." Circumcision, then, took place on the eighth day, and the Apostle, writing to the Colossians, gives its spiritual significance thus: "Putting off the body of the sins of the flesh" (2:11), a consequence of new creation in Christ Jesus (Eph. 2:10). Again, seven days were occupied with the consecration of the priesthood, and on the eighth day they entered upon their work (Lev. 8:33). With the cleansed leper, too, the eighth day marked a new beginning, for on that day he was presented by the priest before the Lord

(Lev. 14:10, 11). The eighth Psalm announces the new kingdom, the kingdom of Christ, "crowned with glory and honor," and with "all things put under His feet (cf. Heb. 2:5-9).

Again, in Luke 9 the Lord Jesus talks to His beloved disciples of His coming sufferings, and then of a day when the Son of Man "shall come in His own glory and in His Father's, and of the holy angels" (v. 26). In the next verse, He speaks of "the kingdom of God." Then follows the transfiguration of the Lord in the presence of Peter, John, and James, who were privileged to see an outshining of that predicted glory. Verse 28 says that this took place about "an eight days after," beginning as it were a new age, when "He received from God the Father honor and glory" (2 Pet. 1:17). It was, moreover, on the eighth day, "the last day, that great day of the feast," that Christ gave utterance to that wonderful invitation to men to a new experience and life: "If any man thirst, let him come unto Me and drink" (John 7:37).

On the first day of the week, that is the eighth day, the seeking women stood by the empty tomb in the garden, and heard the amazing words: "He is not here: for He is risen, as He said. Come, see the place where the Lord lay" (Matt. 28:6). The eighth day had ushered in the new, the resurrection life. Significant, too, it was that the risen Lord, having appeared to His disciples while Thomas was not with them, appeared to the whole company again "after eight days" (John 20:26), and thus gave new life to the faith of the doubter.

13

The Numeral Nine

This is the last of those single numerals known as digits, beyond which we have merely combinations of those previous digits. It, therefore, marks the end. It is the number of finality or judgment. But nine is also three times three, and three signifies Divine completeness. Hence nine denotes finality in Divine things.

In Leviticus 25:22, old fruit was commanded to be eaten until the ninth year, while at the Feast of Tabernacles, on the fifth day, nine bullocks were sacrificed (Num. 29:26). In the prophecy of Haggai, the judgments of God are enumerated in nine particulars: "I called for a drought upon the land, and upon the mountains, and upon the corn, and upon the new wine, and upon the oil, and upon that which the ground bringeth forth, and upon men, and upon cattle, and upon all the labor of the hands" (1:11). Nine persons are recorded in the Scriptures as having been stoned: the blasphemer (Lev. 24:16); the Sabbath-breaker (Num. 15:36); Achan (Josh. 7:25); Abimilech (Jud. 9:53); Adoram (1 Kings 12:18); Naboth (1 Kings 21:10); Zechariah (2 Chron. 24:21); Stephen (Acts 7:59); and Paul (Acts 14:19).

When the Lord Jesus had exercised His

healing power upon ten lepers, only one returned to thank Him, so that He asked this question, "Where are the nine?" (Luke 17:17). At His crucifixion, the ninth hour was marked by the cry of the Holy Sufferer: "My God, my God, why hast Thou forsaken Me?" (Mark 15:34). In Acts 3:1, it was the ninth hour, the hour of prayer, when Peter and John made their way to the Temple. At this prayer-hour, too, God dealt with the seeking Cornelius in a vision (Acts 10:30).

In 1 Corinthians 12, verses 8 to 10, the original gifts of the Spirit are set forth in their completeness, being nine in number: "To one is given by the Spirit the word of wisdom; to another the word of knowledge by the same Spirit; to another faith by the same Spirit; to another the gifts of healing by the same Spirit; to another the working of miracles; to another prophecy; to another discerning of spirits; to another divers kinds of tongues; to another the interpretation of tongues."

Lastly, in Galatians 5:22, 23, are enumerated the component graces collectively described as "the fruit of the Spirit," which is nine-fold: "The fruit of the Spirit is love, joy, peace, long-suffering, gentleness, goodness, faith, meekness, self-control." Displaying these and increasing in them, the believer brings forth fruit unto God.

14

The Numeral Ten

The numeral ten is the beginning of a new series of numbers. From 0 to 9 completes one cycle, and beginning again we put 1 before each number to form a new cycle. Accordingly, ten denotes the perfection of Divine order. But this Divine order implies responsibility for man, and so ten denotes man's responsibility toward God.

Man is possessed of ten fingers and ten toes, speaking of his capacity for action and walk. But capacity implies responsibility, and responsibility brings corresponding judgment or reward, all of which is conveyed by the numeral ten. In Genesis 1 the words "God said" occur ten times, speaking of man's responsibility in the presence of God's Word. Noah completed the antediluvian age in the tenth generation from God, when the judgment fell. Pharaoh's responsibility is brought out in Exodus 9 and the succeeding chapters, in that ten times he hardened his heart, and there followed a like number of judgments.

The ten commandments (Ex. 20) contain all that is necessary to man in number and order, and so measure man's responsibility in walk before God. In the Tabernacle, too, we read of ten curtains, ten pillars, and ten sockets. The silver sockets, too, which formed the foundation of the Tabernacle were ten by ten, speaking of complete redemption. In Numbers 14:22, it is recorded that ten times the children of Israel tempted Jehovah, expression of the people's failure in responsibility. Again, tithes, or one part out of ten, were demanded by God from Israel, this being the measure of their responsibility. In the Scriptures there are ten recorded observances of the Passover: in Egypt (Ex. 12); in the wilderness (Num. 9:5); on the Plains of Jericho (Josh. 5:10); Hezekiah's (2 Chron. 30:1); Josiah's (2 Chron. 35:1); Ezra's (Ezra 6:19); when the Lord was taken at the age of twelve years (Luke 2:42); John 2:13; John 6:4; and Matthew 26:2.

Again, Antichrist's world power is composed of the ten kingdoms symbolized by ten toes on the feet of the image of Nebuchadnezzar's dream (Dan. 2:41), and by the ten horns of the fourth Beast of Daniel's vision (Dan. 7:7). In the parable of the ten virgins, responsibility is enforced (Matt. 25).

The parables of the Kingdom are ten in number in Matthew's Gospel, seven in chapter 13 and three in chapters 22 and 25. In Luke 15:8, this thought of completeness is again indicated in the ten pieces of silver and the anxiety of the loser to find the missing piece.

Finally, in Romans 8:38, 39, is declared the ten-fold security of the child of God through faith in Jesus Christ: "I am persuaded that neither death, nor life, nor angels, nor principalities, nor powers, nor things present, nor things to come, nor height, nor depth, nor any other creature, shall be able to separate us from the love of God which is in Christ Jesus our Lord."

15

The Numeral Eleven

The numeral eleven is not of frequent occurrence in the Scriptures, appearing some thirty-eight times in all. It is more than ten, which speaks of complete order; it is also less than twelve, which denotes Divine government. Accordingly, eleven signifies disorder, imperfection, and incompleteness of earthly government.

In Genesis 32:22, we read of the eleven sons of Jacob, telling of the disorder so prevalent in that family, for later it could be said that "one is not." There were eleven dukes of Edom (Gen. 36:40-43), the near relation and prominent foe of Israel, yet very different from it in order and government. Joseph, the outcast, spent eleven years in Potiphar's house, while the dream that had provoked the jealousy of his brothers spoke of eleven stars (Gen. 37:9). In the Tabernacle were eleven curtains of goats' hair (Ex. 26:7). From Horeb to Kadesh-Barnea, that journey fraught with such great disaster to the people of Israel, was an eleven days' journey (Deut. 1:2). It was short of the land of promise, and of the complete administration of God's laws, by one day.

Eleven cities are mentioned in Joshua 15:51,

and Jehoiakim and Zedekiah each reigned for eleven years (2 Kings 23:36 and 24:18). Eleven kings and rulers were offended with God's servants for witnessing to the truth: (1) Pharaoh (Ex. 10:28); (2) Balak (Num. 24:10); (3) Jeroboam (1 Kings 13:4); (4) Ahab (1 Kings 22:27); (5) Naaman (2 Kings 5:12); (6) Asa (2 Chron. 16:10); (7) Joash (2 Chron. 24:21); (8) Uzziah (2 Chron. 26:19); (9) Jehoiakim (Jer. 26:21); (10) Zedekiah (Jer. 32:3); and (11) Herod (Matt. 14:3).

Matthew 20:6 deals with the eleventh hour, while Matthew 28:16 tells of a meeting between eleven disciples and their Lord. The life of the Lord Jesus Christ upon earth was about thirty-three years, that is, three times eleven. He was the manifestation of God, yet was cut off in the midst of His days (Dan. 9:26), and "we see not yet all things put under Him" (Heb. 2:8).

In Acts 1:26, we have the eleven apostles, incomplete in their testimony, adding to their number a twelfth, "of those men which have companied with us all the time that the Lord Jesus went in and out among us" (v. 21).

16

The Numeral Twelve

Twelve is the numeral of manifest sovereignty. It speaks of the administration of Divine government on the earth. Because it is Divine government it is perfect government. Twelve, therefore, is the symbol of governmental perfection, just as three is of Divine perfection, seven of spiritual perfection, and ten perfection of order, or ordinal perfection.

In Exodus 15:27, the people of Israel, after a trying experience in the desert of Shur, found refreshment and strength at the twelve wells of water at Elim. Twelve precious stones adorned the breast-plate of the High Priest, each stone bearing the name of a tribe (Ex. 28:21). When, after much wandering, the Israelites at last crossed the Jordan and entered the land, the goodness of God in holding back these waters of judgment, and in bringing them into the new life of the promised land, was commemorated by a twelve-stoned monument in the river-bed, and a similar one by the river, at Gilgal (Joshua 4:8,9). Again, twelve oxen bore up the molten sea of Solomon's Temple (1 Kings 7:25), while the twelve gates of the city (Ezek. 48:31-34) speak of Israel's administrative authority among the nations.

At the age of twelve, Christ was found among the doctors at Jerusalem (Luke 2:46). In Matthew 19:28, He predicts a day when He, the Son of Man, shall sit in the throne of His glory, and promises that His apostles "shall sit upon twelve thrones, judging the twelve tribes of Israel." When, later, at His betrayal, He rebuked the impetuous Peter on his resort to force, it was with this question: "Thinkest thou that I cannot now pray to my Father, and He shall presently give me more than twelve legions of angels?" (Matt. 26:53). The very perfection of angelic power was at his disposal, even when He submitted Himself to the hatred of men. In Acts 7:8, Stephen speaks of the twelve patriarchs.

Finally, in Revelation 21 is described "that great city, the holy Jerusalem, descending out of heaven from God" (v. 10). With its twelve gates, twelve angels, twelve names of tribes, twelve foundations, and twelve precious stones, names of the twelve apostles, and its measurement each way of twelve thousand furlongs, it symbolizes the government of the glorified saints over creation.

17

The Numeral Forty

The numeral forty has for its meaning trial. It is the period of full probation, of complete testing.

So under the economy of Israel, manhood was attained at forty years, Isaac and Esau both being married at that age. For forty years, Moses dwelt at the court of Pharaoh (Acts 7:23), then for forty years kept the flocks in Midian (Acts 7:30), while for the last forty he led the children of Israel towards the land of promise. He was forty years learning to think he was somebody, then forty learning he was nobody, after which probation periods he was a fit instrument to be used of God. Again, when the people had encamped under Mount Sinai, Moses was forty days and forty nights in the mount, prior to receiving the two tables of testimony from the hand of God. Later, arriving at Kadesh-Barnea, they were allowed of God to pursue the course they desired (Deut. 1:22), and to send spies into the land, who for forty days and forty nights explored its countryside (Num. 13:25). For these forty days of unbelief, they had to spend forty years in the wilderness, learning the lessons of obedience and dependence upon God, that He might humble and prove them (Deut. 8:2).

In Deuteronomy 25:3, the number of stripes that could be inflicted upon a wrong-doer was limited to forty, while a like number was set apart for an Israelite mother's purification (Lev. 12:2-4). Saul, king of the people's choosing, reigned the probationary period of forty years, as did 'also David and Solomon. In Ezekiel 4:6, the iniquity of the house of Judah is to be borne for forty days, while in 29:13, God judges Egypt forty years.

The Lord Jesus endured the concentrated onslaught of Satan in temptation for forty days (Luke 4:2); for a like period, after His resurrection, He appeared among His disciples, showing Himself to be truly alive by "many infallible proofs" (Acts 1:3).

18

The Perfections of Christ

Jesus Christ, the Eternal Son of God, being the Perfect One, and seven being the numeral in the Scriptures indicative of perfection, it is to be expected that this number should be prominent in God's Word with regard to His Son. The following references will make plain that such is the case.

First, consider·some of the means employed by God—the types—to foretell the worth and work of Christ. Immediately the people of Israel were redeemed out of Egypt, and had entered upon their wilderness journey, provision was made for their worship of the God who had redeemed them. To this end the Tabernacle was erected to a God-given plan, complete in every detail of its furnishings. Between the door of the outer court and the Shekinah light in the Holiest of All, the Lord Jesus Christ in all His redemptive fullness was presented in a seven-fold picture thus: (1) Entering, we reach the Brazen Altar, type of Christ in Regeneration. (2) Next comes the Laver, picture of Christ in Purification. (3) Coming to the Golden Candlestick, we see Christ in Illumination. (4) At the Table of Shewbread, we have Christ in Sustentation.

(5) At the Golden Altar, we consider Christ in Intercession. (6) The Ark of the Covenant presents Christ in Representation, while (7) the Mercy-Seat speaks of Christ in Consecration. Thus is set forth the work of the Lord Jesus Christ in all its wondrous perfection. Again, in the seventh month was the Day of Atonement (Lev. 16:29). On that day the blood was sprinkled on the Mercy-Seat eastward, once only, being Godward. But before the Mercy-Seat it was sprinkled, not once, but seven times, this being to the people the full testimony of perfect atonement (Lev. 16:14).

Moreover, there were seven different sprinklings of blood on that great Day of Atonement: (1) It was sprinkled on the Mercy-Seat (Lev. 16:14); (2) before the Mercy-Seat (Lev. 16:14); (3) before the veil (Lev. 4:17); (4) on the horns of the Golden Altar (Ex. 30:10); (5) on the horns of the Brazen Altar (Lev. 16:19); (6) round about the Brazen Altar (Lev. 16:18); and (7) the blood that was left was poured out at the foot of the Brazen Altar (Lev. 4:18). In this seven-fold way was declared the perfection of the cleansing-power of the precious blood of Christ.

In Isaiah 11:2, the character of the Son of God is declared in these words: (1) "The Spirit of the Lord shall rest upon Him, (2) the spirit of wisdom, (3) and understanding, (4) the spirit of counsel, (5) and might, (6) the spirit of knowledge, (7) and of the fear of the Lord." This seven-fold description depicts the perfection of the One who is "made unto us wisdom" (1 Cor. 1:30), in whom "are hid all the treasures of wisdom" (Col. 2:3), even "Christ the power of God and the wisdom of God" (1

Cor. 1:24). Again, in 2 Kings 5:14, the seven-fold washing of the leper Naaman in Jordan's waters points forward to the perfect obedience of faith that brings the perfect cleansing of the blood of Christ.

In the Old Testament, too, certain words, full of meaning, are used in remarkable numerical order. "Mercy-Seat," picture of Christ, the meeting-place of the sinner and God, is used twenty-seven times, or three times three times three, denoting in intensity the manifestation of Divine perfection. "Frankincense," speaking of the matchless fragrance of His life, occurs in fourteen verses, or two times seven, the witness that He was God's spotless Lamb. "Shittim wood," type of Christ's humanity, is found twenty-eight times, or four times seven, for He was perfectly Divine as well as perfectly human. And last, "Manna," picture of the true Bread from Heaven, is employed fourteen times, or two times seven, speaking of the One who perfectly satisfies both God and man.

At His birth, too, His perfection is marked by this same number seven. In the Old Testament the expression, "These are the generations of" occurs thirteen times. Matthew opens his Gospel with such an expression: "The book of the generation of Jesus Christ," making the number fourteen, or two times seven. The Son of God, born into the world, begins a new creation, and makes the perfect completion of the Works of God. In the same first chapter are these words: "So all the generations from Abraham to David are fourteen generations; and from David until the carrying away into Babylon are fourteen generations; and from the carrying

away into Babylon unto Christ are fourteen generations" (v. 17). Thus with a three-fold repetition of twice seven is it declared that the Son of God was born into the world in the fullness of time, in the perfection of the purposes of God.

Consider now the genealogies of Jesus Christ, which are given in two of the Gospels only, in accordance with the Divine purpose. The clarion note of Matthew is, "Behold thy King" (Zech. 9:9); that of Mark "Behold My Servant" (Is. 42:1); of Luke, "Behold the Man" (Zech. 6:12); and of John, "Behold your God" (Is. 40:9). But a servant needs no genealogy, and God, the Eternal One, has none; hence Mark and John do not give one. Instead, Mark gives God's testimonial to His perfect Servant, "Thou art My beloved Son in whom I am well pleased" (Mark 1:11); while John takes us to the One who was before all, the Inhabitant of eternity, the mighty God: "In the beginning was the Word, and the Word was with God, and the Word was God" (John 1:1). On the other hand, a genealogy is desirable to a man, but essential to a king, hence Luke and Matthew each give one. Again, these differ, not in discord, but in complete harmony, for Matthew, tracing the King, descends by the royal line through Solomon, the king, while Luke, tracing the Man, ascends by the natural line through Nathan, Solomon's elder brother.

Moreover, in Luke's genealogy are seventy-seven names, with God at the one end and His Son, Jesus, at the other, thus stamping the perfect Man with the perfection of Deity. In that of Matthew's account, forty-two generations are given, or six times seven. It has been pointed out that of these, forty-one names are mentioned by Matthew, four are omitted—Ahaziah, Joash, Amaziah, and Jehoiakim—and these, with the twenty-one names before Abraham, make a total of sixty-six. The Lord Jesus Christ was, therefore, sixty-sixth in the line through Solomon, thus sealing His perfect Humanity. Thus does He bear the stamp of the perfection of Divinity, and the perfection of Humanity, in one and the same Blessed Person.

We now turn to a consideration of His life as He tabernacled amongst men. What was He in His own Person? The words of James 3:17 aptly describe Him who was the supreme manifestation of wisdom, its very embodiment: "But the wisdom that is from above is first pure, then peaceable, gentle and easy to be entreated, full of mercy and good fruits, without partiality and without hypocrisy." Such was Christ, who was the wisdom from above.

(1) Was He pure? He was "holy, harmless, undefiled" (Heb. 7:26). (2) Was He peaceable? "Consider Him who endured such contradiction of sinners against Himself" (Heb. 12:3). (3) Was He gentle? "When He was reviled, reviled not again; when He suffered, he threatened not" (1 Pet. 2:23). (4) Was He easy to be entreated? "They constrained Him, saying, 'Abide with us: for it is toward evening, and the day is far spent.' And He went in to tarry with them" (Luke 24:29). (5) Was He full of mercy and good fruits? "He was moved with compassion on them" (Matt. 9:36). This same expression is used of Him five times, all in Matthew and Mark, five being symbolical of grace, or of weakness, here of grace going out to weakness with hands full

of help. (6) Was He without partiality, or, as the marginal reading has it, without wrangling? "He answered him to never a word" (Matt. 27:14). (7) Was He without hypocrisy? He "did no sin, neither was guile found in His mouth" (1 Pet. 2:22). Blessed, spotless Son of God, He was the seven-fold perfection of wisdom.

At the outset, the mission of the Lord Jesus Christ was sealed by this seven-fold sign of the perfection of its origin and purpose. Rising in the synagogue at Nazareth, He took the book of Isaiah, and read from it these words, as recorded in Luke 4:18,19: "(1) The Spirit of the Lord is upon Me, (2) because He hath anointed Me to preach the gospel to the poor; (3) He hath sent Me to heal the brokenhearted, (4) to preach deliverance to the captives, (5) and recovering of sight to the blind, (6) to set at liberty them that are bruised, (7) to preach the acceptable year of the Lord." Marvelous perfection of compassion, grace, and power! He, and He alone, is the complete answer of a presently-silent Heaven, to every need of man.

Again, during His life upon earth, seven occasions are mentioned of angels, messengers of God, appearing either to or concerning Him. (1) At His birth it was an angel who reassured the fearful shepherds, saying: "Fear not, for, behold, I bring you good tidings of great joy, which shall be to all people. For unto you is born this day in the city of David, a Savior, which is Christ the Lord" (Luke 2:10, 11). (2) When the cruel Herod sought His life, an angel appeared to apprise Joseph of the fact, and to counsel flight to Egypt (Matt. 2:13). (3) Later, when this Herod was dead, an angel appeared once more to Joseph, directing him to return again to the land of Israel (Matt. 2:19). (4) In the wilderness, when He had resisted every onslaught of the Tempter, "angels came and ministered unto Him" (Matt. 4:11). (5) Again, on that eventful betrayal night, when at a stone's cast from His sleeping disciples, He agonized with God in prayer, "there appeared an angel unto Him from heaven, strengthening Him" (Luke 22:43). (6) On that glorious triumph morning, the morning of His resurrection, it was the "angel of the Lord" who, at the empty tomb, brought terror to the enemies of the Lord, the keepers, and comfort to the friends of the Lord, the seeking women (Matt. 28:2-5). (7) Finally, when, with hands uplifted characteristically in blessing, He was taken up, and the enveloping cloud received Him out of the sight of His still-gazing followers, it was "two men in white apparel" who inspired them with new hopes as they foretold His coming again (Acts 1:10, 11).

Further, when, at the request of His disciples, He taught them to pray, He did so in a seven-fold petition, expressing the perfection of request; and when He unfolded the nature of His kingdom it was by seven parables (Matt. 13).

Moreover, John's Gospel, which was written that we might believe that Jesus is the Christ, the Son of God, records seven miracles. In chapter 2, the water is turned into wine; in 4:47-50, the nobleman's son is raised; while in 5:4, the man at the Pool of Bethesda finds health. Chapter 6 tells of the wonderful feeding of five thousand; in 9:1-7, a blind man is made to see; in chapter 11, Lazarus is raised from the dead;

and in chapter 21 is the record of the wonderful draught of fishes. Thus in the manifestation of perfect power is it declared that Jesus was indeed the Christ, the Son of God.

In the same Gospel is found a record of Christ's gifts, which also are seven in number, for He was ever the perfect Giver. (1) He gives His flesh,—"The bread that I will give is My flesh" (John 6:51). (2) He gives His life,—"I am the Good Shepherd: the Good Shepherd giveth His life for the sheep" (John 10:11). (3) He gives also an example to His own of loving, lowly service,—"I have given you an example, that ye should do as I have done to you" (John 13:15). (4) Then, through His prayer to the Father, He gives the Comforter, the Holy Spirit,—"I will pray the Father, and He shall give you another Comforter" (John 14:16). (5) Again, knowing the tribulation awaiting His own, He gives them abiding Peace,—"Peace I leave with you, my peace I give unto you" (John 14:27). (6) Foreseeing a day in the which men would not abide the truth, but would challenge His very utterances, He gave us His own Words, with the assurance that they were inspired of God,— "I have given them the words which Thou gavest Me" (John 17:8). (7) And last, this same Person, who poured upon His people the abundance of His grace, gave them, too, His glory,—"The glory which Thou gavest Me, I have given them" (John 17:22). His gifts, therefore, bear the stamp of Divine Perfection.

Several words, too, by their repetition, are worthy of note. In the book of Revelation, the word "Lamb," a peculiar word used of the Lord Jesus Christ, occurs, with reference to Him, twenty-eight times, or four times seven, denoting the perfection of His sacrifice.

This sinless Son of God sinful men rejected and nailed to a tree, yet in the hour of His suffering His very words were characterized by this perfect number, for from those gracious lips fell seven utterances: (1) "Father, forgive them; for they know not what they do" (Luke 23:34). (2) "Verily, I say unto thee, 'Today shalt thou be with Me in paradise'" (Luke 23:43). (3) "Woman, behold thy son! . . . Behold thy mother!" (John 19:26,27). (4) "My God, My God, why hast Thou forsaken Me?" (Matt. 27:46). (5) "I thirst" (John 19:28). (6) "It is finished" (John 19:30). (7) "Father, into Thy hands I commend My spirit" (Luke 23:46).

Further, in His resurrection, and later in His ascension glory, this same seven marks with perfection all pertaining to Him. He was the stone which the builders rejected, yet seven times is it declared that it is now become the Head of the corner. Again, twenty-one times, or three times seven, is He spoken of as being at the right hand of God,—the perfection of exaltation. He is declared seven times to be a High Priest after the order of Melchizedek, thus proclaiming the perfection and abiding character of His work of intercession for His people.

How highly God has honored His beloved Son can only be measured by the depth of the humiliation that was His. Thus, in Philippians 2, each is described in a seven-fold way. In wondrous condescension the Lord Jesus (1) "made Himself of no reputation, (2) and took upon Him the form of a servant, (3) and was made in the likeness of men; (4) and being found in fashion as a man, (5) humbled Himself, (6) and became obedient unto death, (7) even the death of the cross (v. 8). But when man and the devil had done their worst for Him, God did His best, and so follows a seven-fold exaltation, for we read: (1) "Wherefore God also hath highly exalted Him, (2) and given Him a name which is above every name, (3) that at the name of Jesus every knee should bow, (4) in heaven, (5) in earth, (6) and under the earth, (7) and that every tongue should confess that Jesus Christ is Lord, to the glory of God the Father" (9:11) .

Again, this honor given Him of His Father is seen in the seven-fold title used concerning Him in the Epistle to the Hebrews. In 1:2, He is the "Heir of all things." In 2:10, He is the Captain of our salvation. Chapter 3:1 calls us to "consider the Apostle" of our profession. Chapter 5:9 tells us He is the Author of salvation. In 6:20, He is the Forerunner, entered within the veil. In 10:21, He is a "High Priest." Lastly, in 12:2, He is the "Author and Finisher of faith."

In the same book, in which the eternal glories of Christ are contrasted so fully with the transient glories of the Jewish ritual, it is fitting that seven blessings accruing to the believer should be mentioned, all flowing from Him who is the "better Hope" (7:19), and all likewise described as "better." In 7:22, we have a better testament; 8:6, better promises; 9:23, better sacrifices; 10:34, a better substance; 11:35, a better resurrection; 11:16, a better country; and, in 11:40, a better thing.

Moreover, the relationship into which Christ has brought the Church with Himself is stated in Ephesians 5 in a seven-fold way: (1) "Christ is the Head of the Church" (v. 23). (2) "The Church is subject unto Christ" (v. 24). (3) "Christ also loved the Church." (4) "And gave Himself for it." (5) "That He might sanctify and cleanse it with the washing of water by the Word." (6) "That He might present it to Himself a glorious Church, not having spot, or wrinkle, or any such thing." (7) "But that it should be holy, and without blemish" (vv. 25-27). That this blessed design will be completely accomplished is borne out by the seven-fold use of the word *amomos*, meaning "without": "without blemish" (Eph. 5:27 and 1 Pet. 1:19); "without spot" (Heb. 9:14); "without fault" (Rev. 14:5); "without blame" (Eph. 1:4); "faultless" (Jude 24); "unblameable" (Col. 1.22).

In Ephesians 4:4-6 is stated a seven-fold unity that characterizes this Church, while in Colossians 3:12-13, and again in 2 Peter 1:5-7, are seven graces that should be true of every member of that Church. Last, in the book of Revelation, where the number seven predominates, the Name of names, Jesus, is repeated just seven times, Jesus Christ a like number, and Lord twenty-one times, or three times seven, all symbolical of His intrinsic perfection. And when John beheld the vision of His glory, he saw a host before Him, "and the number of them was ten thousand times ten thousand, and thousands of thousands," all united in ascribing to the Son of God this seven-fold praise: "Worthy is the Lamb that was slain to receive power, and riches, and wisdom, and strength, and honor, and glory, and blessing" (Rev. 5:12).

Finally, when he saw gathered round His

throne "a great multitude, which no man could number, of all nations, and kindreds, and people, and tongues," again heaven re-echoed to this seven-fold chord of praise: "Blessing, and glory, and wisdom, and thanksgiving, and honor, and power, and might, be unto our God for ever and ever. Amen" (Rev. 7:12).

19

Arithmetical Accuracy

Before closing this little book, it is deemed desirable to say something on the accuracy of the Word of God. This is displayed, with the utmost mathematical precision, in many instances throughout its pages.

In Genesis, chapter 12, God appeared to Abraham, to lead him out from Haran to a land which He promised to give him, saying: "I will make of thee a great nation" (v. 2). Abraham obeyed and went out, and yet no son was born in whom the promise might be fulfilled. Time passed, and Abraham prospered, yet in his prosperity did not forget God, but was still submissive to His will. Lot might make personal choice, but Abraham was happy to take God's choice for him. Once again God appeared to him (Gen. 13:16), and confirmed His promise, saying, "I will make thy seed as the dust of the earth: so that if a man can number the dust of the earth, then shall thy seed also be numbered." Time continued to pass, with yet no son, but Abraham still pursued the path of faith, refusing to become involved in material affairs with Sodom's king. God signified His pleasure with him by a third meeting, and a third repetition

of the promise (15:4), saying: "He that shall come
forth out of thine own bowels shall be thine
heir." Years ran their relentless course, and
Abraham was now ninety-nine years old, and
still the child of promise was not born. But now
the purpose of God has matured, and the
promise is fulfilled: "Sarah conceived and bare
Abraham a son in his old age, at the *set time* of
which God had spoken to him" (Gen. 21:2). The
comment of the Holy Spirit upon this is found
in Hebrews 11:12: "Therefore sprang there even
of one, and him as good as dead, so many as
the stars of the sky in multitude and as the sand
which is by the seashore innumerable." But this
Isaac was only a type of the Lord Jesus Christ,
the true Child of Promise. According to the
reckoning in our Bibles, Christ was born into
the world about the four-thousandth year, or
fortieth century.

Forty, we have seen, is the symbol of
probation. So after a full period of the world's
probation under law, Jesus Christ was born into
the world to usher in grace. Further, as Isaac
was born when Abraham was one hundred
years old, and as good as dead, so Christ came
to the world when all flesh was seen dead in
the eyes of God. Truly, the God of heaven has a
"set time," which is always fraught with
meaning, nor does it ever outrun or lag behind
the event.

In Numbers 11:5, another picture is presented
to us. The people of Israel, redeemed from the
land of the taskmaster, are making for God's
land of promise, "a good land and a large" (Ex.
3:8). On the way, however, they have the woeful
experience of tiring of the food of God's

providing, and of longing again for that of the land of bondage. With no recollection of their sorrows in that land, of the brick-making without straw, or of their groans and sighs, they recall only the pleasant things, the food it offered them. The items given, fish, cucumbers, melons, leeks, onions, and garlic, make six in all. But six is man's number, denoting failure, insufficiency of abiding satisfaction. Here it speaks of the vanity and disappointing nature of all that pertains to man, the "restless, unsatisfied longing" that lies deeply embedded in the human heart. Byron portrays it in these lines:

"Though wit may flash from fluent lip, and mirth
    distract the breast,
Through midnight hours that yield no more then
    former hope of rest;
'Tis but as ivy-leaves around the ruined turret wreathe,
All green and wildly fresh without, but worn and grey
    beneath!"

Contrast this with Deuteronomy 8:8, where the food of Canaan is detailed: "A land of wheat, and barley, and vines, and fig trees, and pomegranates; a land of olive oil and honey." Here the items are seven in number, stamped with the mark of Divine perfection, the guarantee of unalloyed satisfaction. Of a truth, "They shall be abundantly satisfied with the fatness of Thy house; and Thou shalt make them drink of the river of Thy pleasures" (Ps. 36:8).

The accuracy of the Holy Scriptures finds another verification in 2 Kings 2. Elijah, about to be taken up into heaven, leaves Gilgal, and, accompanied by Elisha, goes to Bethel, then to Jericho, and finally across the Jordan. Turning to his companion, the departing prophet says:

"Ask what I shall do for thee, before I be taken away from thee" (v. 9). Note the response of Elisha: "I pray thee, let a double portion of thy spirit be upon me." This request was fulfilled in a remarkable way, for Elijah in his lifetime had performed eight miracles, whereas Elisha was used to perform sixteen! His was "a double portion:"

One more example of the unerring accuracy of God's arithmetic is found in the words of Genesis 8:4. In chapters 6 to 8 is recorded the story of God's early judgment upon the earth, and His gracious provision for Noah, who "found grace in the eyes of the Lord" (6:8), Who could therefore say of him, "Thee have I seen righteous before Me" (7:1). Entering into the Ark, which he prepared to the saving of his house, Noah, shut in by the hand of God, passed through the waters of judgment which enveloped a sinful world. In 8:4 are these suggestive words: "And the ark rested in the seventh month, on the seventeenth day of the month, upon the mountains of Ararat." What necessity is there to be so explicit as to the exact day? Turn to Exodus, chapter 12, where God speaks to Moses and Aaron in these words: "This month shall be unto you the beginning of months: it shall be the first month of the year to you" (v. 2).

Now, what month was it in reality? It was the seventh month, henceforth to be known as the first month. Then follows the choosing of an unblemished lamb, its preservation and examination from the tenth until the fourteenth day, and then its being killed in the evening of that fourteenth day. This lamb was the passover lamb; the occasion, that memorable first passover. Now pass in thought through many years. Again the first month of the year, the former seventh month, has come round. Again the feast of the passover, on that fourteenth day, has come. It is a more memorable one than ever before, for Calvary's Lamb, the Lamb of God, is there. Watch the mob, as, fully armed, they come to the lonely garden over the brook, and take Him prisoner. He is taken on that fourteenth day. On the next, the fifteenth day, a solemn day, they nail Him between the thieves, "on either side one, and Jesus in the midst." When the following day dawns, the Lord of Heaven, the Prince of life, is held in the bonds of death. Then comes the next, and seventeenth day, of that first month, formerly the seventh. And what then?

> "Death cannot keep his prey,
>   Jesus my Savior,
> He tore the bars away,
>   Jesus my Lord!"

"The birth-pangs of death gave birth to the Living One" (Acts 2:24), for He "rose again the third day, according to the Scriptures" (1 Cor. 15:4).

But what connection has this with the ark that Noah built to God's plan? Let these, the words of a last-century preacher, answer: "What is the ark of old to us, but an emblem of His full redemption? He is the one deliverance from all peril. He is the heaven-born refuge. He is the all-protecting safety. He is the building of enduring life; the foundation of which was laid in the counsels of eternity; which was reared in the fullness of time on the plains of earth; and the head of which towers above the skies. He is that lofty fabric of shelter, which God decreed, appointed, and provided, and sets before the sons of men. He is that sure covert, which is so fortified that all the thunder-bolts of the almightiness of Divine judgment play harmless around it; and all the raging storms of vengeance, all the fury of the waves of wrath, only consolidate its strength. It must be so. For our hiding-place is the mighty God. Our salvation is Jehovah's Fellow. Our glorious Sanctuary is the glorious Jesus" (Henry Law).

What, then, is the significance of that simple statement in Genesis 8:4: "The ark rested in the seventh month, on the seventeenth day of the month, on the mountains of Ararat"? Just this.

As the ark, bearing Noah and his family, passed in perfect safety through those judgment waters, and on the seventeenth day of the seventh month touched the new world; so our Ark, the Lord Jesus Christ, blessed for ever, passed through the floods of the wrath of God at the place which is called Calvary, and came forth into a new world, the resurrection life, on the anniversary of that very day. And the believer, perfectly sheltered in Him, in Him passed through judgment, and in Him is risen in newness of life, into the resurrection world; for indeed "old things are passed away; behold, all things are become new" (2 Cor. 5:17).

The Word of God makes no mistakes. Spanning even the centuries, it is accurate to the very day. The mighty God caused to be set forth the glories and excellencies of His Son in a multitude of events and objects beforehand, with the same perfect precision as He afterwards recorded them in words.

Concerning that same passover day, Sir Robert Anderson writes: "The yearly Passover was merely a memorial of the Passover in Egypt; and the midnight agony in Gethsemane was the great antitype of that midnight scene when the destroying angel flashed through the land of the Pharaohs. And as His death was the accomplishment of His people's deliverance, it took place upon the anniversary of 'that self-same day that the Lord did bring the children of Israel out of the land of Egypt.' And that day again was a great anniversary; it was 'the self-same day' of the covenant with Abraham."

Such are the marvelous workings of Him Who said: "I am God, and there is none like Me, declaring the end from the beginning, and from ancient times the things that are not yet done, saying, 'My counsel shall stand, and I will do all My pleasure'" (Is. 46:9, 10).

20

Reading to Profit

We have seen that although the Holy Scriptures consist of sixty-six books, they are not a mere collection of miscellaneous writings. On the contrary, they form one logical whole, an organic unity, which is both living and life-giving. As befits their Author, God the Holy Spirit, they are perfect in their completeness, weakened by no omissions, and burdened by no redundancies. The Person, who is the glorious central theme of their teachings, is none other than Jesus Christ, the eternal Son of God. When the purposes of God the Father had ripened, He, "the Word," perfect expression of the thoughts of God manwards, "was made flesh and dwelt among us" (John 1:14). He, who had ever been perfect in His Divinity, now assumed the perfection of Humanity. In doing this, He surrendered not the most infinitesimal part of either, but was at one and the same time very God and yet very Man. By His perfect Humanity, the Lord Jesus Christ was able completely to know our need, while by His perfect Divinity He was able completely to meet it.

As it was with the "Living Word," so is it with the "Written Word." Clothed in the lan-

guage of men, set forth in incidents and circum-
stances that fit wholly into the lives of men, it is
truly human, and is therefore adapted to our
need. But that which was clothed in the lan-
guage of men was the very Breathing of God,
and, being Divine, is consequently absolutely
unerring, and so is the one foundation upon
which men can confidently build, the one guide
along the unknown vista of life, the one light in
the darkness amidst a multitude of will-o'-the-
wisps.

Carlyle, the rugged sage of Chelsea, depicts
man as a "wanderer upon the face of the earth,
standing before the Sybil-cave of destiny, and
calling into it question after question, to find no
answer but an echo." But there is an answer, if
men would but seek it in the right direction.
That answer is the Bible, the Word of God. The
world's vast library holds many books for the
varied moods of men. God's one Book is perfectly adapted for all moods. In its universal
application, His Word is again found to re-
semble His Works. One writes: "How many
ends does God accomplish by one single element! Air supplies the lungs, supports fire, con-
veys sound, reflects light, diffuses scents, gives
rain, wafts ships, evaporates fluids, and fulfills,
besides, I know not how many other purposes.
Man, from his infirmity, makes a special tool
for every purpose. God uses one thing for many
purposes" (Jukes). His one revelation is compe-
tent to suit man in each of his varied needs, for
His "Word is true from the beginning" (or,
"from the first word"; Ps. 119:160).

That it is abundantly adequate for the varied
requirements of humanity is made clear from

twelve symbols which are used to depict its functions. These twelve together form a seven-fold purpose, thus expressing perfection of supply and resource. (1) The Word of God is a mirror (Jas. 1:23-25). Looking therein, we see ourselves as God sees us, and also as God would make us. (2) When we have apprehended something of our state before God, His Word is a Laver (Eph. 5:26), where our sin may be washed away. (3) Hitherto we have been spiritually dead (Eph. 2:1), and the Word of God is a seed (1 Pet. 1:23), which the Holy Spirit quickens to beget new life within us. (4) Now that we have been brought into the way of God, we need to be guided therein. To this end, it is a Lamp and a Light (Ps. 119:105). (5) But that spiritual life needs to be sustained, to be strengthened, and to be satisfied. The Bible is the God-appointed and sole means for this three-fold purpose, being spoken of as Bread (Jer. 15:16), as Milk and Strong Meat (Heb. 5:12), and as Honey (Ps. 19:10). (6) Again, the grace of our Lord Jesus Christ is such that, though He was rich, yet for our sakes He became poor, that we through His poverty might be rich (2 Cor. 8:9). The source of real and abiding wealth to the believer is the Word of God, which is described as Fine Gold (Ps. 19:10). (7) Moreover, the child of God, through faith, is not only a son, but a servant, and a soldier, and as such needs to be equipped for the work and warfare of the Christian life. To supply this equipment, God's Word is a Fire, a Hammer (Jer. 23:29), and a Sword (Heb. 4:12). Thus richly endowed, the simplest child of God lacks no good thing.

The relation of man to the universe around

him is two-fold. He tills the ground, and extracts from it food to support life in the greatest degree of comfort. But man also surveys the immeasurable expanse of the heavens, and finds moral uplift and food for thought in contemplating its vastness and untold wonders. Similarly, the Word of God provides an inexhaustible store of food to nourish and upbuild the spiritual life of the believer, yet displays a boundless canopy sparkling with the glories of grace, which, gazing at, we may wonder, till wonder is transformed into worship.

Comparing the works of man with those of God, Andrew Jukes well says: "Man's work, if we are continually poring over it, will soon weary us, a little attention will in time make us masters of it. God's work, the more we examine and look into it, will only attract us the more. The more it is studied, the more it opens out, at every step unfolding fresh and endless objects. Take any portion of it,—the earth, the air, the sky; and the further we search, the deeper we examine, the more are we led to acknowledge that as yet we know next to nothing, and that the great ocean of truth of every kind lies before us, as yet all unfathomed and unfathomable." So is it with God's Word. But as the gold-mine yields its precious metal only to the toil and application of the digger, so the limitless wealth of the Scriptures is enjoyed only at the cost of diligent search. To ensure that the believer may successfully pursue this quest, the Holy Ghost has left on record four words for our guidance.

In John's Gospel, chapter 5, and verse 39, is found this injunction, "Search the Scriptures." A venturesome cub, during the absence of the lioness, wanders from the lair, and is lost in the undergrowth. No sooner does the mother miss her young than she sets out in quest of it. Examining carefully the ground, she notices footprints of the wanderer. These she diligently follows, till at length she finds the object of her quest. Such is the significance of this word, "Search!"

Again, in Psalm 1 are found these words: "In His law doth he meditate day and night" (v. 2). Picture the patient cow, which, having nibbled the luscious grass all over the meadow, now lies down to rest. Then she begins to feed in the true sense of the word. Withdrawing the food from that first stomach where it is stored, the cow proceeds in leisurely fashion to masticate the grass thoroughly, extracting the last drop of sweetness from it. Animals possessing this power we call ruminants. That is what the Holy Spirit asks us to be when He employs this word "Meditate!"

Thirdly, writing to the Corinthian believers, the Apostle Paul, through the Spirit, uses this phrase: "Comparing spiritual things with spiritual" (1 Cor. 2:13). The first law a child learns in arithmetic is that he can only work with terms of the same "name." Only as he observes this elementary fact can he successfully apply the four rules. To attempt to explain God's Word by man's thoughts, and from man's viewpoint, is to commit a breach of this elementary law, and to court disaster. Spiritual things are not apprehended by natural ability, but are spiritually discerned (1 Cor. 2:14). The best enlightenment upon Scripture is that given by its Author, the Holy Spirit. Hence, He urges the believer to compare "spiritual things with spiritual." There is a fourth word, found in the Epistle of James: "Whoso looketh into the perfect law of liberty" (1:25).

Watch the scientist as he examines some tiny organism. Placing it under the glass of his microscope, he turns the little wheel until the instrument is in proper position, adjusts the focus, then gazes long and intently at the wonderful details displayed. That is what we are invited to do with God's Word, when the Holy Spirit says, "Whoso looketh into!"

As we thus search, and meditate, compare, and look into the pages of the inspired Record, while the illuminating power of the Holy Spirit shines full upon them, we shall not fail to see clearly therein the gracious Person of Jesus Christ our Lord. And seeing Him, it must follow as the night the day, that we shall be irresistibly drawn to Him, while the alluring earth-ties will loosen their hold. The experience of these lines will then become a blessed reality:

What doth strip the seeming beauty
   From the idols of the earth?
Not a sense of right or duty,
   But a sight of peerless worth.
'Tis that look that melted Peter;
   'Tis that face that Stephen saw;
'Tis that heart that wept with Mary,
   Can alone from idols draw;
Draw, and win, and fill completely,
   Till the cup o'erflows its brim.
What have we to do with idols,
   Since we've companied with Him!